Special Education in Change

Special Education in Change

edited by
Mel Ainscow

David Fulton Publishers
in association with the Cambridge Institute of Education

David Fulton Publishers Ltd
2 Barbon Close, London WC1N 3JX

First published in Great Britain by
David Fulton Publishers 1989,

© Cambridge Institute of Education

British Library Cataloguing in Publication Data

Special education in change.
   1. Special education
   I. Ainscow, Mel
   371.9

   ISBN 1-85346-127-X

Typeset by Chapterhouse, Formby
Printed in Great Britain by BPCC Wheatons Ltd, Exeter

Contents

Preface

I have a notice in my office which says, 'If you don't like my book write your own'. In a sense that is what the authors of the chapters in this book have done. As practising teachers they have carried out research into aspects of their work and then presented their findings in a way that is of interest to others involved in similar fields. In other words, this is a book written by practitioners for practitioners.

No doubt this material will be particularly valuable to teachers on advanced courses who need to complete dissertations. For them it provides a wealth of suggestions and examples as to how research can be undertaken in applied settings. However, it is also important to recognise that the studies presented are not detached from the day-to-day life of schools. They provide a clear indication of how school-based inquiry can be used as a means of facilitating improvements in policy and practice.

I must take this opportunity to acknowledge the contribution of my colleagues at the Cambridge Institute of Education. In particular I must thank the Director, Howard Bradley, for his encouragement and support; Barbara Shannon who helped to formulate the idea for this book; Colin Conner, David Hopkins, Peter Holly and Martyn Rouse for sharing ideas; and Ann Sargeant who never complains when she has to type from my horrible handwriting.

Finally I must pay tribute to the authors who have contributed chapters. They are to be congratulated on writing their own book.

Mel Ainscow
Cambridge
June 1989

CHAPTER 1

Special Education in Change: Themes and Issues

Mel Ainscow

This book has three broad aims. They are:

(1)   To illustrate the nature of the changes that are occurring in the field of special education;
(2)   To provide some examples of how these changes can be investigated; and
(3)   To show how teacher research activities can inform the development of practice.

The text grew out of the work undertaken by experienced teachers enrolled on various award-bearing courses at the Cambridge Institute of Education.

In reading the ten subsequent chapters that form the core of the book, readers should be aware of four themes that permeate the text. These themes, which give a certain cohesion to what on the surface appear as a range of diverse pieces of writing, are as follows:

(1)   The nature of the changes that are occurring in the field of special education.
(2)   The impact these changes are having across the various sections of the education service.
(3)   The need to develop methods of inquiry that have the breadth and flexibility to inform the development of practice.
(4)   The importance of teachers as 'reflective practitioners', skilled and confident in learning from their own experience.

The purpose of this introductory chapter is to provide an explanation of these four themes and, in so doing, raise issues that form the agenda of debate for the rest of the book.

The nature of the changes

The last ten years or so have seen considerable changes in special education. These are based upon a growing awareness of the need for a reconceptualisation of what the term special education means (Skrtic, 1986). Indeed, they are part of an argument that ultimately questions the existence of special education as a separate area of concern (Ainscow and Tweddle, 1988; Stainback and Stainback, 1984; Wang et al., 1986).

Traditionally, special education was seen as a specialised wing of the education system that took responsibility for the education of a designated group of children. The assumption was that because of their disabilities or limitations these children required forms of education different from that offered to the majority. The aim was to provide forms of teaching that would overcome the problems of the children.

The obvious outcome of this perspective was the existence of special schools and classes where arrangements were made for groups of children seen as sharing similar problems. In addition, further provision was made in many primary and secondary schools for groups of children said to be in need of remedial education.

This orientation has been questioned on a number of levels. For example:

● Despite the good intentions of those involved in providing special education, it can be seen as a strategic ploy to exclude children thought likely to disrupt the smooth running of schools (Tomlinson, 1982).
● The nature of the educational experience provided for children in special provision is often characterised by narrowness of opportunity (Ainscow, 1989).
● It is based upon a process of labelling. This involves grouping children together on the basis of a number of shared characteristics, which, as a result, tends to encourage the creation of stereotypes that are to the disadvantage of the children involved (Booth, 1988).
● Convincing evidence of the efficacy of such approaches is not available (Hallahan et al., 1988; Leitch and Sodhi, 1989).

The reconceptualisation of special education that is gradually becoming accepted is based upon a very different analysis of the nature of educational difficulty. Rather than assuming that problems arise solely as a result of the limitations or disabilities of children, it recognises that they occur because of the interaction of a range of different factors. Some of these factors are within children but others are of an environmental nature, particularly in relation to the forms of teaching that are provided.

This change of perspective, sometimes referred to as an interactive perspective (Wedell, 1981), requires special educational needs to be defined relative to particular educational contexts. In other words, educational difficulties are seen as being context bound, arising out of the interaction of individual children with a particular educational programme at a certain moment in time.

Whilst being somewhat complex, this definition has the advantage that it tends to encourage a sense of optimism. Unlike the traditional approach where the focus on child-centred causes of educational difficulty tended to create an air of despondency, the interactive perspective focuses attention on a range of factors that teachers can influence to encourage children's learning. It emphasises the fact that what teachers do, the decisions they make, their attitudes, the relationships they develop and their forms of classroom organisation, are all factors that can help children to experience success in school. By the same argument, of course, these factors can also help to *create* educational difficulties for some children.

Implications of the changes

This changing approach to special education has major implications for the organisation of schools and the work of teachers. In particular it has implications for provision made in ordinary schools. It argues for the development of primary and secondary schools that are responsive to children with a wide range of needs (Thousand and Villa, 1989; Wang *et al.*, 1986). Indeed special education, instead of being seen as a search by specialists for technical solutions to children's problems, becomes a curriculum challenge shared by all teachers within every school.

As a result of this type of argument, many local education authorities and schools have been reviewing their policies and practices in recent years. In many cases the aim is to move towards what has come to be called 'a whole school approach' to special educational needs. The idea is that all teachers within a school accept responsibility for the development and progress of all its pupils.

In many primary schools these developments have led to the

appointment of members of staff to act as coordinators for special needs. Their responsibility is to support colleagues as they attempt to respond to the needs of all the children in their classes. Similarly in secondary education many traditional remedial departments have been replaced by arrangements that emphasise cross-subject support. Inevitably these changes have also had a significant impact on the various special education support agencies and, of course, on special schools.

Across the whole range of provision the changes that are taking place have specific implications for the work of individual teachers, particularly those perceived as being specialists. Many teachers who traditionally spent much of their time working with small groups of children withdrawn from regular lessons for intensive instruction in basic skills now find themselves having to work collaboratively with colleagues in seeking more generalised curriculum approaches. In special schools, also, teachers may be required to work more closely with colleagues in mainstream education, either providing support or working collaboratively on joint curriculum initiatives (Ainscow, 1989).

This account sounds positive, rational and encouraging. It gives the impression that the education service is marching in unison towards new ways of working with agreement and understanding. Alas, this is far from being the case.

As is usual with significant change, the service as a whole is finding it very difficult to come to terms with the new version of special education. At a national level, documents from the Department of Education and Science encourage confusion between traditional and newer perspectives, whilst at local authority level the implementation of policies based on interactive perspectives is in some confusion. This confusion was highlighted recently by the publication of a report by a research team from the University of London as a result of a nationwide survey of policy and practice (Goacher et al., 1988).

Inevitably this general confusion is reflected in the practice of schools. Despite the rhetoric of whole school approaches, traditional views of special education persist and the policies of many schools consist of an uneasy amalgam of old and new. This creates contradictions and tensions that can be a major source of stress for individual teachers.

If the education service is to find a way successfully through this difficult interim phase there is a need for those involved, at all levels, to become clearer about the rationale upon which the new ways of working are based. As we know, change, particularly when it involves new ways of thinking and behaving, is a difficult and time-consuming process. Michael Fullan (1982) argues that, for it to be achieved successfully, a change has to be understood and accepted by those involved. Understanding and acceptance take time and need encouragement.

How then can this be achieved? How can teachers and others involved in the school system be helped to come to terms with the new version of special education? This book argues that one way forward is to encourage teachers to take a more positive approach by learning how to investigate their own practice. The aims are to facilitate understanding and to encourage professional development.

Methods of inquiry

The argument I make in this section is that the reconceptualisation of special education necessitates the use of forms of enquiry that will help teachers to understand the nature and outcomes of the changes that are occurring. Furthermore I will argue that the dominant tradition of research and evaluation is no longer suitable for this task. Consequently there is a need to accept the advice of a number of authors who have argued for the adoption of a new approach (e.g. Barton, 1988; Iano, 1986; Schindele, 1985).

Traditionally, research and evaluation in the field of special education have been influenced by theories derived from educational psychology. This was largely consistent with special education being seen as a search for solutions to solve a technical task. As a result the aim was to establish, through carefully controlled experiments, the existence of generalised laws that teachers could use as a basis for their interventions. Indeed, much of teacher education, particularly with respect to special education, was based upon this type of thinking. Teachers attended courses to learn about theories derived from research in order that they could then use these to inform the development of their teaching.

The emphasis within this dominant research tradition is on the use of experimental research designs of a statistical type. These involve the study of the relationship between sets of variables with a view to making generalisations that can be applied across settings. So, for example, research might consider the impact of teachers' use of praise upon the social conduct of pupils. The aim would be to demonstrate relationships between the two variables, praise and behaviour, in order to prove the existence of laws that would apply in the classrooms of other teachers.

Such investigations are based upon a number of assumptions. In particular, they assume that variables such as praise and social conduct can be defined in ways that could be said to apply across different settings, times and people. The problem with this is that classrooms are complex places, and interactions between teachers and pupils are unique, so that such generalised interpretations are always subject to doubt.

As long as special education was framed as a series of technical tasks concerned with finding solutions to the problems of groups of children said to share similar problems, this dominant research tradition seemed to provide a good fit. Whilst issues of methodology, not least to do with rigour, continued to encourage argument, the idea of seeking to establish laws of cause and effect that could be used to make generalisations about classroom life seemed appropriate.

As I have argued, however, the reconceptualisation of special education places far greater attention on the individuality of children and, significantly, the uniqueness of particular contexts. The concern is with particular children as they interact with particular contexts at a given time. The idea of establishing predictions across people, time and contexts is, therefore, to say the least inappropriate. Rather what is needed is a deeper understanding of the nature and outcomes of particular educational events and situations. In this sense reality is seen as something that is created in the minds of people involved in an event or situation rather than something that can be defined objectively, observed systematically and measured accurately.

In the light of this argument, what are needed are forms of inquiry that:

- Have the flexibility to deal with the uniqueness of particular educational occurrences and contexts;
- Allow schools and classrooms to be understood from the perspectives of different participants; and
- Encourage teachers to investigate their own situations and practice with a view to facilitating improvements.

Teachers as reflective practitioners

In recent years a number of tutors at the Cambridge Institute of Education have emphasised the idea of teachers as researchers within their courses. In addition, the Institute has a long tradition of work in the field of action research.

In collaboration with my colleagues, particularly Colin Conner, Peter Holly and Martyn Rouse, I have been encouraging teachers involved in special educational needs courses to carry out school-based inquiries. Within this work the use of methods of inquiry that meet the criteria mentioned above is emphasised. In particular, course participants are introduced to approaches that will be useful in their everyday work. Indeed, the overall aim is to encourage teachers to see themselves as 'reflective practitioners', skilled in learning from their own professional experiences (Schon, 1983). Consequently the studies they undertake tend to take the form of investigations or case studies of aspects of their own practice.

This work has been influenced by a number of groups of writers, including those concerned with the idea of the teacher as researcher (e.g. Bell, 1987; Hopkins, 1985; Stenhouse, 1975; Walker, 1985), the action research movement (e.g. Elliott, 1981; Kemmis and McTaggart, 1981), and evaluators and researchers who base their work on the notion of naturalistic inquiry (e.g. Lincoln and Guba, 1985; Merriam, 1988; Skrtic, 1985; Woods, 1986). Across this diverse literature a number of common themes emerge that influence our work on school-based inquiry at Cambridge. They are as follows:

(1)   Forms of inquiry are used that allow the researcher to examine particular events or processes as a whole and in their natural settings.
(2)   Research designs are seen as being emergent. That is to say, the directions and forms of an investigation are decided upon as information is collected.
(3)   The human being is seen as the primary 'instrument' for gathering information.
(4)   Use is made of whatever methods of inquiry seem appropriate. However, the main emphasis is on qualitative methods, particularly participant observation and interviewing.
(5)   Through processes of data analysis and interpretation, theories emerge from information that is collected. This is usually referred to as 'grounded theory' in that it is seen as being grounded in the data (Glaser and Strauss, 1967).
(6)   Accounts are usually presented as case studies with, where possible, some attempt to suggest tentative applications of the findings to other settings.

Chapter 12 provides some notes on methods of inquiry and suggestions for further reading.

Overview of the chapters

The ten subsequent chapters were written by teachers as a result of undertaking school-based investigations based on the ideas discussed in this chapter. All of them are summaries of much larger studies submitted as part of an award-bearing course. In providing their accounts some of the authors emphasise the outcomes of their investigations whilst others prefer to focus on the processes involved.

The chapters are examples of what I hope will become a new tradition of inquiry in the field of special education one that emphasises the idea of teachers taking responsibility for investigating their own practice with a view to making improvements.

For purposes of convenience the chapters are grouped on the basis of their setting. The first two are set in primary schools. Pauline Schiff describes some of the findings of her investigations into the development of policies for meeting special needs in a primary school. It is a striking example of how individual teachers are having difficulties in coming to terms with new ways of thinking about special education. Lilias Reary is also interested in school development. Her account looks at the development of policy as a result of an in-service education programme.

Chapters 4, 5 and 6 are set in secondary schools. Steve Cooke examines his role as coordinator for special needs. In her chapter, Susan Marsh looks at pupil and teacher perspectives of a differentiated curriculum. In a similar way, Geraldine Callaghan outlines her theory of effective classrooms as a result of observations and interviews carried out with pupils and teachers.

The next three chapters are about the work of special schools. Dave Hewett is the headteacher of a special school and he argues for the importance of action research as a means of facilitating curriculum development. Steve Cochrane summarises a detailed study of schools where pupils with physical disabilities are integrated and draws out implications for policy development. In Chapter 9, Brian Steedman describes the evolution of a project to introduce cooperative learning in a special school for pupils with emotional and behavioural difficulties.

The final two chapters are written from the perspective of teachers fulfilling advisory roles. Barry Ainsworth describes the work of a group of support teachers developing more flexible and responsive approaches to assessment. In Chapter 11, Andy Redpath presents suggestions for successful support work based on his evaluation of the work of one teacher.

In reading these ten chapters it should be remembered that the authors are *not* professional researchers. They are all busy teachers who have found time to investigate important issues in the field of special education. In so doing they have also, in my view, acquired skills that should enable them to become more successful teachers.

References

Ainscow, M. (1989), 'Developing the special school curriculum: where next?', in D. Baker and K. Bovair (eds), *Making the Special School Ordinary?* (London: Falmer).

Ainscow, M. and Tweddle, D. A. (1988), *Encouraging Classroom Success* (London: Fulton).

Barton, L. (1988), 'Research and practice: the need for alternative perspectives', in L. Barton (ed), *The Politics of Special Educational Needs* (London: Falmer).

Bell, J. (1987), *Doing Your Research Project* (Milton Keynes: Open University).

Booth, T. (1988), 'Challenging conceptions of integration', in L. Barton (ed), *The Politics of Special Educational Needs* (London: Falmer).

Elliott, J. (1981), 'Action research: a framework for self-evaluation in schools' (Cambridge Institute of Education, mimeo).

Fullan, M. (1982), *The Meaning of Educational Change* (New York: Teachers' College Press).

Glaser, B. G. and Strauss, A. L. (1967), *The Discovery of Grounded Theory* (Chicago: Aldine).

Goacher, B., Evans, J., Welton, J. and Wedell, K. (1988), *Policy and Provision for Special Educational Needs* (London: Cassell).

Hallahan, D. P., Keller, C. E., McKinney, J. D., Lloyd, J. W. and Bryan, T. (1988), 'Examining the research base of the Regular Education Initiative', *Journal of Learning Disabilities*, 21 (1), 29–35.

Hopkins, D. (1985), *A Teacher's Guide to Classroom Research* (Milton Keynes: Open University).

Iano, R. P. (1986), 'The study and development of teaching: with implications for the advancement of special education', *Remedial and Special Education*, 7 (5), 50–61.

Kemmis, S. and McTaggart, R. (1981), *The Action Research Planner* (Victoria: Deakin University Press).

Leitch, D. A. and Sodhi, S. S. (1989), 'The remediation hoax', in M. Csapo and L. Goguen (eds), *Special Education Across Canada* (Vancouver: Centre for Human Development and Research).

Lincoln, Y. S. and Guba, E. G. (1985), *Naturalistic Inquiry* (Beverly Hills: Sage).

Merriam, S. B. (1988), *Case Study Research in Education* (London: Jossey-Bass).

10

Schindele, R. A. (1985), 'Research methodology in special education: a framework approach to special problems and solutions', in S. Hegarty and P. Evans (eds), *Research and Evaluation Methods in Special Education* (Windsor: NFER – Nelson).

Schon, D. (1983), *The Reflective Practitioner* (New York: Basil Books).

Skrtic, T. M. (1985), 'Doing naturalistic research into educational organisation', in Y. S. Lincoln (ed), *Organizational Theory and Inquiry* (Beverly Hills: Sage).

Skrtic, T. M. (1986), 'The crisis in special education knowledge: a perspective on perspectives', *Focus on Exceptional Children*, 18 (7), 1–15.

Stainback, W. and Stainback, S. (1984), 'A rationale for the merger of special and remedial education', *Exceptional Children*, 51, 102–11.

Stenhouse, L. (1975), *An Introduction to Curriculum Research and Development* (London: Heinemann).

Thousand, J. S. and Villa, R. A. (1989), 'Accommodating for greater student variance in local schools', Paper presented at 1989 CEC Convention, San Francisco.

Tomlinson, S. (1982), *A Sociology of Special Education* (London: RKP).

Walker, R. (1985), *Doing Research: A Handbook for Teachers* (London: Methuen).

Wang, M. C., Reynolds, M. C. and Walberg, H. J. (1986), 'Rethinking special education', *Educational Leadership*, 44, 26–31.

Wedell, K. (1981), 'Concepts of special educational needs', *Education Today*, 31, 3–9.

Woods, P. (1986), *Inside Schools* (London: RKP).

CHAPTER 2

The Development of Provision for Meeting Special Education Needs in a Primary School

Pauline Schiff

The aim of the research described in this chapter was to look in detail at the way in which special educational needs are being met in a primary school. As the special needs teacher attached to the school, I hoped to gain an insight into my colleagues' definitions of special educational needs, and how they set about dealing with them.

The definition of special educational needs that informs this study is relative and interactive. This view implies that there is no absolute definition of special needs that can be applied to a child regardless of her/his educational environment. Rather, special educational needs may occur when there is a gap between what the child can do and what s/he is expected to do. In other words, special educational needs can be defined as an interaction between what the child brings to the educational environment and what the educational environment provides for the child. From this perspective, teachers' understandings and definitions of special educational needs, and the consequent provision within the classroom and within the school, are of central importance. If special educational needs are to some extent 'constructed' by teachers and by the school, I wanted to discover whether there exists within the school a common understanding of special educational needs. I also wanted to discover whether such definitions were shared between the school and its LEA.

A further aim of my research was to look at the potential for educational change within the school. I wanted to gauge the extent to which colleagues felt involved in defining proposals for change in the area of special needs, and the extent to which meaning about such change was shared.

Research strategy

I set about gaining data for my research by conducting taped interviews with six class teachers and with the head. My reasons for choosing this method of data collection were as follows: first, from a practical point of view it was not possible to take time off from a full-time teaching commitment to undertake methods of inquiry that would require me to spend time in other teachers' classrooms observing and/or recording what was going on; second, some teachers, when presented with a questionnaire by another member of staff, had expressed reservations about the possibility of adequately expressing all their thoughts and feelings in writing; third, I hoped that the interview, if it was fairly open-ended, would provide class teachers with an opportunity to talk about how they perceived special educational needs in their class – I hoped to gain some insight into their understanding of the situations they were in; finally, the interviews themselves could perhaps be of practical use, both to the class teacher and myself, in terms of planning future special educational needs input, and this was indeed the case in two of the interviews.

The interviews took place at various times of the day – four during the lunch hour, two after school (in school) and one in the evening at my home. It was not possible, from the point of view of time, to interview all the teachers in the school, so half were chosen, and it seemed more likely that a balance of views would be obtained if, of those six, three were teachers receiving a regular input from the special needs teacher and three were not. The purpose of the interviews was explained and the interviewees were asked if they were willing to be taped. By taping the interviews rather than taking notes I hoped to record more accurately what teachers were actually saying. They all agreed. Shortly after the completion of the interviews a transcript of the interview was given to each interviewee, who was then free to make any alterations that s/he felt necessary.

The account presented in this short chapter is a summary of the key issues that emerged from the investigation.

Defining special educational needs

Intro to policy.

The philosophy behind this research is the belief that teachers' views of special educational needs are essential to any policy that aims to meet these needs. For it is the teacher who will define, or not define, a need and it is the teacher who will attempt, or not attempt, to meet that need.

The Warnock Report (DES, 1978) introduced the concept of a continuum of special educational needs, which 'relates to the need which any individual child may be seen to have for assistance, support and intervention in order to pursue an educational programme'. This continuum of need has to be seen within the relative context of the child's class and school, for, if the 'learning environment' is sympathetic and geared towards meeting individual needs, there will be fewer special educational needs. And there is no break in the continuum; since, as Dessent (1987) suggests, 'if an individual child is picked out from the continuum as being, in some sense, deserving of particular special attention in terms of, say, specialist teaching, individualised help or additional staffing, there will always be a child not so regarded, who is only marginally dissimilar in terms of need.'

It is this arbitrary, relative nature of defining a child's needs that is of importance, because of the implications in terms of teachers' practice and school policy. It was with a view to gaining an understanding of teachers' definitions of special educational needs and how they feel they are meeting them, that the interviews were carried out.

All the class teachers were asked the same opening question:

> 'Are there any children in your class you are concerned about, and if so, what are your concerns?'

After the opening question the interview followed the train of thought of the interviewee, with questions being put in order to get her to elucidate or expand on certain points.

The six teachers interviewed offered their own definitions of special educational needs as follows

> 'If I put a label on a child as being special educational needs, they won't remain special educational needs . . . it's a floating thing . . . that at particular times some children may have special educational needs . . . Always aware that the very gifted children have got special educational needs and they always will have – and equally at the other end – with children like Z . . . he, throughout most of his school life, will have special educational needs . . . and there are those in the middle

that you've always got to have an eye on . . . at some point they're going to have them in some area.'

'I . . . do identify some children in my own mind as having special educational needs . . . like X . . . children who need five hundred times the stimulus or help to achieve what others would achieve more quickly . . . A, B, C, and D need much more time to pick things up. X is weird. Those four are quite a bit slower.'

'Coming in as their new teacher . . . what I saw was a lot of children with individual difficulties and individual needs, and I still see them that way. I find it very difficult to specify children who have greater needs than others, which is what I assume you are interested in . . . I have no very low achievers.'

'F has very little English. She goes to C (the multi-cultural teacher) once or twice a week . . . she needs lots of opportunity to talk . . . Most other children seem to be progressing fairly well, obviously some very, very fast and others very gently, but nevertheless they're showing progress, so I don't really have any – not real – worries about the others . . . Obviously there are children who are slower, but there are none who are significantly slower . . . I really can't see anybody who's not making some progress. They're a pretty bright bunch really.'

'I prefer to think that children don't have special educational needs . . . the difference between individual needs and special educational needs – the whole class have individual needs. So special needs does become synonymous with concern for the kids who are failing by comparison with the others. Certain children are giving absolute cause for concern. I feel that everyone else is moving along OK.'

'In the ideal world I'm concerned about all of them at different times. So we get down to a definition of – in your sphere – special need. There are some children who have specific obvious difficulties and they come into different categories – behavioural difficulties, intellectual problems – those are the two main areas. Nobody with a physical disability . . . I have three children who are slow if you look at a test score . . . they do have specific intellectual difficulties. I'm thinking of spelling and handwriting in particular . . . I have a child I would consider a slow learner – as I understand the phrase – not remedial. Had a handwriting problem. Also had emotional problems at home . . . '

Another thread, common to most of the interviews, was a statement of how the special educational needs identified by the teacher were being met or how, ideally, she would like them to be met:

'The children we singled out at the beginning of the year, I'm quite happy about them now. And also the ones I felt weren't being stretched at the beginning of the year, I feel we're catering for them too... I consider that the children the special educational needs teacher works with – both the 'slow' group and the 'bright' group – are the children I consider to have special educational needs.'

'The children identified at the beginning of the year as having special educational needs are not those I am currently concerned about, because the special educational needs teacher is seeing them...'

'The boys with the more overt behaviour problems are the ones who get attention in class. It isn't that I don't consider the girls, it's that I feel the boys get in the way of everybody's development and I think that's a problem I really must tackle... I'm hanging back and learning about the children and the teacher's perceptions – before I do anything.'

'I would like F to get more input from the multi-cultural teacher, so she can acquire the language she needs... she needs small group work with another teacher, in a quiet corner – there are difficulties with withdrawal and yet the classroom is so small.'

'I would always welcome a second opinion on kids... it would be good to have two class teachers... it's your assessment of those children, whatever way you do it... are we all assessing children in the same way? We have to have some sort of standard thing. We could perhaps benefit from more structured observation from another person in the classroom, not formal assessment... If you were in the classroom, say three days a week, frequent contact with a lot of kids, then I'm sure we'd pick up on a lot of things. When you work with them in a group you can see their levels of thinking and identify any gaps in the progression of their thinking.'

'I would love to have the children one to one at some time during the week because they have specific things about them that I need to get to the bottom of... J is not a slow learner. Remedial... would benefit from precision teaching... I would like some time to stretch K. I feel that he needs special provision one to one... L lacks confidence in her own ability, suffers from low self-esteem, needs this extra special attention.'

Having interviewed six of the class teachers, I then interviewed the head. I asked him how he saw special educational needs being met in the school.

'An umbrella system really. Starts off with the class teacher. Under that is the special needs teacher and under that is the parent. And the ancillaries should come somewhere in the middle of that . . . the main body has to be carried by the class teacher . . . hopefully they'll feed into you if they want information and advice and you'll extract, and underneath that has got to be you with the class teacher liaising with the parents.'

I also asked him to list the key aspects of a policy that he thought would meet special educational needs.

'Parental   involvement . . . early   identification . . . record   keeping . . . and the special educational needs teacher. A resource that is the special educational needs teacher, to deal with some of the kids, not only from a withdrawal point of view but also so that the class teacher has someone to refer to, that's very reassuring, who can confirm their opinion or who can gently give them suggestions, resources, etc. that they wouldn't otherwise know about. It is reassuring for the class teacher to discuss children she is worried about with a teacher . . . and to try to raise teachers' awareness of the problems some of those kids must have . . . increase sensitivity . . . to look behind the kid, to handle him fairly and firmly, but to recognise his problems, to understand him, and as his class teacher there isn't always time to do this. If the kid thinks the teacher is understanding, or on their side, you get a better response from them.'

Data analysis and interpretation

When analysing the data I had collected it became clear that, in terms of teachers' definitions of special educational needs, there was little acceptance of an interactive concept of special educational needs. Teachers see the difficulties as being within the child, whether intellectual, emotional or behavioural. The difficulties may be long-term or short-term, but the teachers are thinking in terms of pupils they perceive to have learning difficulties and who they perceive as being, to a greater or less extent, 'deficit models'.

What is noticeable by its absence from the interviews is any feeling that the teachers themselves might play a part in creating needs as well as in meeting them. There is no mention of the need to examine curriculum provision to see whether certain difficulties could be prevented.

The concept of the relativity of special educational needs is reflected in some of the teachers' comments, as is the idea of a continuum of need. As one teacher put it, special educational needs become synonymous with concern about a child's progress and this concern is in relation to other children's progress in the class. However, the idea that a child's special educational needs are relative not only to other children but also to the educational environment is less apparent. Focusing as they did on the importance of meeting all children's individual needs, the majority of the teachers interviewed did reflect the principle laid down in the Warnock Report that all teachers are teachers of children with special educational needs.

Although they were not asked to comment directly on the role of the special educational needs teacher, most of the class teachers interviewed made some allusions to this during the course of the interview. The concept of the special educational needs teacher put forward by current writers in the field (see, for instance, Dessent, 1987; Bines, 1986) – namely a consultant, an adviser, an agent of change who works more with the teacher than with individuals or small groups of children with special educational needs – was largely absent from their comments.

The head's views can be seen to correspond fairly closely with those of the class teachers. He sees special needs as being 'within-child', and often due to emotional disturbance. He does not identify the curriculum as either a potential cure or a potential cause of children's learning difficulties. His emphasis is to look behind the child, rather than behind the educational environment, when seeking to meet special educational needs.

From the interview data collected it can be seen that the class teachers and the head have a shared understanding of the concept of special educational need. They see that need as a difficulty the child brings to school. The practical support provided by the special needs teacher, whether she takes the class or whether she withdraws one child with learning difficulties, is an attempt to deal with a difficulty that is specific to that child or those children; there is no 'knock-on effect' on to general curriculum provision.

This shared understanding within the school does not exist between the school and its LEA. For the LEA, following the 'new relativity' (Goacher et al., 1988) of the definition of special educational needs introduced by the 1981 Education Act, is concerned to implement change in schools. The LEA is concerned that schools develop whole school policies that will recognise the crucial role of the curriculum not only in 'curing' learning difficulties but also in preventing their occurrence. One means of implementing this change was to appoint special needs teachers to area special education teams, train them, and then place them in selected ordinary schools.

Comment and recommendations

It is my belief that successful educational change does not just happen. Teachers' views and their subjective understanding of the situation they are in need to be taken into account at each stage of the process of change, so that the meaning of innovation can be shared by all participants.

From the research carried out in this study, I would suggest that certain conditions need to be fulfilled if there is to be successful change in meeting special educational needs in the school. These are:

● Written guidelines from the LEA, which would make clear the authority's view of special educational needs in ordinary schools and the direction in which the LEA would like these schools to develop.
● Regular meetings in school with officers of the LEA who are involved in policy-making in the area of special educational needs.
● Time should be set aside within normal teaching time for teachers to meet regularly to discuss special educational needs within the school as a whole. If time for discussion is created, then teachers are more likely to feel part of the ongoing process of change, and, consequently, successful change is more likely to take place.

The research I undertook made clear to me the gap that exists between teachers' perceptions of special educational needs and how they should be met, and the LEA's policy for meeting special educational needs in ordinary schools. If the school is to become more in line with LEA policy, then greater attention should be paid to teachers' subjective views of special needs and to the involvement of teachers in the process of change. Effective provision for special educational needs both starts and ends with the teachers involved.

References

Bines H. (1986), *Redefining Remedial Education* (London: Croom Helm).
DES (1978), *Special Educational Needs* (Warnock Report) (London: HMSO).
Dessent T. (1987), *Making the Ordinary School Special* (London: Falmer Press).
Goacher B. *et al.* (1988), *Policy and Provision for Special Educational Needs: Implementing the 1981 Act* (London: Cassell Educational).

CHAPTER 3

Towards a Whole School Approach: The Effects of a School-Based Project on a Primary School

Lilias Reary

Ambrose (1987) states that 'when the 1981 Education Act set a new framework for restructuring the whole system of special education – wherever possible in ordinary schools — it was clear that a training initiative centred on those teachers in ordinary schools...would be necessary in order to support the policy' (p. 32). Indeed, a large number of one-term courses flourished and by 1984 Moses *et al.* (1987) were able to study 25 such courses, finding that they had four main characteristics – a taught element, a programme of school visits, information on the various support services, and a 'school project', which was the 'key element' in most.

A number of such courses had been organised by Cambridge Institute of Education and, indeed, the commission (project) had been an important part, consisting of individual study and research. This was generally based in the school of the course member. The extent to which this effected change in the school was unpredictable, but in part seemed to be determined by the nature of the project, the general climate within the school and the extent to which the staff were involved.

In the autumn of 1986, Cambridge Institute of Education and two LEAs planned a new initiative that sought to maximise the effect of the school-based project by attempting to develop a 'whole school' response to a perceived need. The project was conceived in three distinct phases. Phase One was the pre-course phase in which the course participants' schools were asked to review their existing policies in special educational needs with a view to agreeing on an area for further development; this area would form the basis of the project. Phase Two covered the period when the course participants were present at the Cambridge Institute of Education – this involved attendance on Fridays over two terms plus a one-week block in each term. During this phase, the course participants were expected to develop, with their colleagues, a response to the project topic in school. Phase Three was the post-course phase in which it was hoped that work on implementing the project would continue.

Having been involved as an LEA tutor on this course, I examined one school's response to the school-based project throughout its three phases. I selected a school in which the outcomes from the project had been successful at the different levels of school, individual and curriculum. These outcomes are particularly interesting as they were completely unexpected at the outset since the school did not appear to have the necessary preconditions for successful INSET. Indeed, the school was almost the antithesis of the innovative school described by Kerry (1985), in that it did *not* have 'structures to facilitate innovation' while the headteacher did *not* 'appear committed to the activity'. Further, the course participant did *not* have a high profile in the staff room.

Such unexpected, positive results warrant closer examination and so I shall briefly describe the context of the school within which the project took place, give a brief outline of the three phases of the project, and then discuss some of the main issues arising, before looking at some of the implications.

Methodology

To obtain data about individual members of staff and to find out the general response to Phase Two, a questionnaire was given to all members of staff at the beginning of Phase Three. In addition, two semi-structured interviews were carried out – one with the course participant and the other with the headteacher.

All this information was supplemented by semi-participant observations made by me during the meeting in Phase One and meetings one and two in Phase Two. Comments were also provided by the visiting teacher in meeting four of Phase Two. Many other informal comments from members of staff were made to me during my regular visits to the school.

The context – the school

The school is a large rural primary school situated in a moderately large village. It caters for children aged from 4 to 11 years. There are recognisable infant and junior departments, containing 13 classes, which are organised on a strict chronological age basis.

At the time of this study the headteacher did not have a class responsibility and had been in post for 16 years. There were 13 members of staff with an average of 19 years' teaching experience and an average of just over 9 years service in the school. During Phases One and Two of the course the deputy head was on secondment to another school, while the language coordinator was on an exchange teaching post. In the previous three years the staff had attended an average of 2.7 courses per person, with six members of staff having attended one or none. One-third of the courses had been two days or less in length.

There had been a major curriculum initiative six years previously when the whole staff, with the help of an advisory teacher of reading, were involved in the selection of a new reading scheme. This involved fortnightly meetings over one academic year. The normal pattern of meetings, however, is one per month, after school. These meetings tend to be largely organisational and administrative in nature – curriculum matters could be discussed, but they would tend to occupy one item on the agenda. There are also separate meetings for junior and infant staff and they are arranged on an ad hoc basis, tending to be of a planning nature.

Phase One of the project

There was a lunchtime meeting of the whole staff so that the nature of the course could be explained. It was not the intention to select an area of study at that moment, but, in fact, a very lively discussion ensued and the staff were in total agreement that they would like to work on a spelling policy. The head did not participate during the meeting but he gave his assent to the chosen topic at the end of the meeting. Later, the head told me that he was very pleased with the high level of staff participation and discussion.

Phase Two of the project

A series of four staff meetings on spelling was timetabled.

Meeting 1

As a preparation for the first meeting the staff were asked to fill in a questionnaire designed to elicit the variety of methods and techniques currently in use in the teaching of spelling in the school. It was designed to be a sharing of ideas – a non-threatening situation.

From the information gathered, four questions seemed to warrant further discussion:

(a) Should spelling techniques be based on a phonic or visual approach?
(b) How should wrong spellings be corrected or, indeed, should they be corrected?
(c) How should correct spellings of words be made more accessible to children?
(d) Is there a link between spelling and handwriting?

The staff enthusiastically debated the first three questions, covering the main arguments found in any learned work on spelling. I was drawn into the debate on several occasions, but the head did not contribute. The head chose to close the meeting before the fourth question was discussed.

The meeting was chaired by the course participant.

Meeting 2

The staff indicated to the course participant that they would like to examine further the look–cover–write–check method. As preparation the staff were given an interim report of an experiment in Fife carried out by Charles Cripps, a tutor at the Cambridge Institute of Education.

Again, the discussion was lively among the staff, but the head did not contribute.

The course participant chaired the meeting.

Meeting 3

Before the meeting, the course participant circulated copies of what she saw as the main points of agreement from Meetings 1 and 2 and these were put up for modification and negotiation during the first part of the meeting.

The staff also brought examples of spelling games that they had gathered over the years, and this led to an agreement to initiate a central resource catalogue.

The course participant chaired the meeting. The head was not present.

Meeting 4

This meeting was largely given over to discussing the link between handwriting and spelling – the fourth question that had been left over from the first meeting.

The stimulus for this meeting was a talk by a practising teacher in a neighbouring school. This visiting teacher commented on the staff's high interest level and also on their level of discussion.

The staff all agreed that this was a most informative and useful session.

Phase Three of the project

The project and the interest it generated were still very much alive and ongoing. Indeed it was one of the items on the agenda for the first Wednesday meeting of the new term. The staff realised that there was still a lot to be discussed and negotiated but they hoped that a policy document could be prepared during the spring term of 1988. Other areas of the curriculum were also being suggested for the whole school to study together in a series of meetings, and the head reported that such meetings would be timetabled once per month on Mondays.

Discussion of key issues

My immediate response was that the above project was extremely successful and that this success must be examined so that the ingredients of success could be identified. The need for such analysis was further emphasised by the course prospectus, which stated that the course evaluation 'will largely depend on whether the school based development projects are judged as being successful'. This latter statement immediately begs two questions that seem fundamental to any evaluation:

● What are the criteria for judging a successful project? (i.e. what is success?)
● Who should the judges be?

A starting point might be to evaluate the series of school-based staff meetings with reference to the choice of subject (i.e. spelling); the presentation of the subject (i.e. the format of the meetings); the content of the meetings; the role of the external course; and the role of the head.

I shall now look at each of these issues in more detail, accepting that the clients (in this case the head and staff of the school) must be the main judges (evaluators).

The choice of subject

The decision to study spelling was the concrete expression of a need perceived by the staff, as a group. Just prior to the Phase One meeting, according to the course participant's project report, a 'frustrated comment' made in the staff room suggested that the new intake of junior pupils couldn't spell even the simplest words. This had made the staff realise that their teaching of spelling was perhaps not as effective as it should be, which perhaps explains why the consensus to study spelling was reached so easily. Thus, to express it in Fullan's (1982) terms, the topic of the meetings was addressing what was seen to be a 'priority' need by the staff themselves and, he believes, such a need is one of the necessary preconditions for successful change. Change, of course, can be equated with INSET as it is usually 'assumed that INSET leads to innovation in schools' (Sebba and Robson, 1987).

From the timing point of view this subject seems to have been most opportune: if the series of meetings had not taken place the topic of spelling could have become an unproductive bone of contention in the staff room. Further, no one had attended an external course in spelling in the previous three years, while five members of staff stated that, prior to the series of meetings, their initial training had been their most important source of knowledge for spelling techniques and four of these teachers had been in teaching for more than 18 years (one had been in teaching for 35 years!).

It was also interesting to note that nine teachers placed 'trial and error' and their own experiences in the classroom among the three most important sources of knowledge for teaching spelling. This is not to be underestimated, as it surely represents a very strong foundation of 'informal' and 'systematic' knowledge, but, as Iano (1986) contends, this knowledge must be harnessed and shared at a more 'public' level (i.e. with the rest of the school) if it is to lead to anything other than serendipity. Thus, there was a reservoir of experience on the chosen subject that was just needing to be tapped.

The head also attributed much of the success of the project to the choice of subject. He believed that the fact the staff had selected the topic themselves was absolutely crucial, and went as far as to say that he knew 'opposition would have been met if the staff had had a topic or series of meetings imposed on them' (as in the Bedford model described by Harnett, 1986).

The format of the meetings

When the course participant and I discussed the format we had four main objectives:

(1) The staff had to be active participants, as all too often, as Alexander (1980) states, teachers have been 'relatively passive receivers of whatever was available' and, indeed, they tend to bring this 'ingrained expectation to school-based courses' (Keast, 1982).
(2) A focus or stimulus should be given out before the meeting as a 'warm up'.
(3) Outside 'experts' would be avoided at this stage, but a practising teacher would be invited to talk about the link between handwriting and spelling.
(4) The format should be flexible enough to respond to interests generated by previous meetings.

The level of discussion and participation throughout the sessions was high and commented on favourably by the head, the course participant and myself. Many of the staff stated that they enjoyed the format and appreciated the pre-meeting hand-outs.

The most memorable meeting, in the staff's view, was the meeting addressed by the visiting teacher. Such practical experience, though readily available, is an underused, if not undervalued, resource, despite the fact that 'there is little doubt that teachers often learn from other teachers' (Bolam, 1982).

The course participant chaired each meeting. The majority of staff seemed to appreciate this continuity and agreed that the course participant was most successful in this role, although she, herself, admits feeling 'terrified at first'.

The content of the meetings

The staff members present at the meetings were asked to rate the series for interest on a four-point scale; and 80 per cent of them found it very interesting or interesting, while the course participant and the head both rated the series as interesting.

The staff were then asked to rate the series on a four-point scale for usefulness, accepting the argument put forward by Sebba and Robson (1987) that 'interesting sessions could be judged not useful, if they are felt to be not professionally relevant'. Seventy per cent of the staff found the series useful or very useful and no one found it useless. The course participant found the meetings gave her a 'lot of useful information', while the headteacher also found them very useful.

The staff were generally agreed that the content of the meetings had allowed them to explore common problems and concerns in the teaching of spelling and also to investigate some possible methods for teaching. The course participant expressed disappointment that, as a staff, they had not yet written a spelling policy (her original objective), but in fact, had she forced the pace of the meetings to achieve this, some of the useful content might have been lost because, as Eraut (1983) points out, 'most school-based INSET tries to do too much too quickly' and as a result runs the risk of being ineffective.

The role of the external course

Although there was general concern about the teaching of spelling in the school, it is generally agreed that the course participant's need to work on a school-based project was the necessary catalyst to get the series of meetings under way.

The course participant stated that she had certainly never regarded herself as an innovator or initiator of change and she would not have taken on this role if it had not been a course requirement. Thus, the external course facilitated change by providing a teacher from within the school with the space, time, support and motivation to organise the series of meetings.

Other members of staff had attended exernal courses, but the effects exercised by the present course were in direct contrast to any of the out-comes from those 36 courses previously attended by the staff of the school over a three-year period. Only on four occasions was there any formal feedback to the rest of the staff and this took the form of two verbal reports as agenda items in the monthly staff meeting and two special staff meetings. From this, it is possible to see why such traditional courses were 'failing to have any significant impact on practice in schools' (Henderson and Perry, 1981). This is not to say that all traditional courses are useless, but 'rather that their utility was limited' to the course attender. Thus, the present course could be described as being designed to extend the utility of external courses.

The role of the head

In setting out guidelines for effective INSET, Sebba and Robson (1987) state that 'the active involvement of the Head Teacher is crucial'. This is a view substantiated by most research and summed up by Powers (1983) when he states that the headteacher holds 'substantial power over the success or failure of any inservice'.

From an observer's view, the head's role in the present study could best be summed up as neutral: he did not prevent the meetings from taking place, but on the other hand he was not overtly supportive. He did not contribute during the meetings and he did not chair the meetings. Several members of staff commented on his apparent lack of support, but happily this did not reduce the staff's enthusiasm for the project.

External appearances can be deceptive, however, as, according to the headteacher, he had carefully thought out his role. He felt that the course participant should chair the meeting as it was 'good, professional experience' and he did not contribute during the meetings so that there could be 'freer discussion'. This, though, is a potentially dangerous course, as Bolam (1982) suggests that the staff could interpret this position 'not as indicating neutrality but as a positive indicator of lack of support'. To avoid such misinterpretation the head should have commenciated his role to the staff or even negotiated his role with the staff.

Further, the head was also giving an element of covert support to the course participant after meetings by commenting favourably to her on the way she had conducted the meetings and on the level of staff discussion. The course participant found this helpful as she was lacking in confidence, but states that she would also have appreciated more overt support.

Much of the above has been largely an historical (i.e. of events past) evaluation or an evaluation of process. It is, of course, important to evaluate the process, as successes in this area will determine any possible future developments. However, the ultimate evaluation must deal with the question, 'Did change take place?' This is the 'outcome' or 'impact' evaluation described by Alexander (1980).

The next section will address this question in terms of teachers as individual practitioners, the course participant, and the school as an institution.

Did change take place?

The teachers as practitioners

Fullan (1982) warns that 'effective change takes time' and that 'lack of implementation is not necessarily because of rejection or resistance'. Nevertheless, four teachers reported that their teaching of spelling had changed in some way since the meetings – this ranged from now linking it with handwriting to concentrating on a more visual approach using the 'Breakthrough to Literacy' folders.

Another teacher responded 'not yet because the meetings I attended indicated a need for a whole school approach and this has not been implemented'. This is obviously a teacher who has understood the broader implications of the series of meetings and I would include her response with the positive responses. Yet another teacher reported that she had not changed any of her methods, but that the meetings had 'helped to pin-point common problems'; surely this identification could be regarded as one of the preconditions for change. Elliott (1978) would certainly regard this as a legitimate process in change, as he believes it is better to get an understanding of the problem before finding a solution. This level of reported change seems very high, especially if it is compared with the degree of change from traditional external courses. It should also be remembered that the degree of change could ultimately be higher as there are going to be further meetings on the topic.

The course participant

The course participant states that her personal and professional self-esteem has risen as a result of the school-based project. She also states that she feels 'much more confident and enthusiastic'. The head has also commented on this increased confidence, while the staff have automatically looked to the course participant to arrange the next series of meetings on spelling.

In addition, the course participant reports that she has changed her approach to spelling.

The school

As reported above, there has been an addition to the regular meetings' programme in the school. The staff liked the forum for discussion that the meetings provided and so agreed with the head to hold curriculum development meetings once per month on a Monday after school. This will allow prolonged study of selected curriculum areas.

What are the implications of this study?

The case study school

The role of the head causes most concern and this must be discussed with him. Certainly, his apparently neutral stance did not prevent a successful outcome this time, but perhaps this neutral role was counteracted by a 'Hawthorn effect' provided by the external course. Thus, further potentially successful INSET projects could be 'at risk' if he does not take a more active, positive stance.

The school staff must receive feedback on the process evaluation so that they can plan interesting and useful in-service meetings in the future. There is obviously a considerable amount of experience and expertise on the staff and this must be utilised constructively and supported by the LEA.

All schools are complex, unique and idiosyncratic institutions, as any ethnographic study reveals, and the above school is no exception; however it is still possible to make some general comments with reference to other schools and to course organisers.

Other schools

Powers (1983) and Sebba and Robson (1987) give guidelines for successful INSET; in the process evaluation this study supports their findings by demonstrating the need for:

- staff negotiation to identify needs;
- careful planning and variety in presentation;
- interesting and useful content;
- formative and summative evaluation.

Further, this present study shows how the external course and the course participant acted as catalysts for the series of meetings. Thus, it would seem useful to designate someone on the staff to take on this role – Kerry (1985) recognises this when he writes: 'there can be little doubt that innovation works best when someone . . . acts as the focus of that change'. Moreover, the external course played an interesting facilitating role, suggesting that school-based and school-focused in-service training or whole school approaches should be outward as well as inward looking. This is accepted by Henderson and Perry (1981) when they state that 'the headteacher and his staff have a critical part to play in planning and executing a school's INSET programme but . . . others must be involved' – I would perhaps modify this to read that others, i.e. outsiders, should be involved on *some* occasions.

Course organisers

As stated in the introduction, Moses *et al.* (1987) refer to the school-based project as being the 'key element' in most of the courses they studied; however, I doubt if its 'spread effect' (in terms of the other teachers it could reach) (Powers 1983) had been realistically estimated or appreciated. It appears from the above case study that the school-based project is a crucial element since, when successful, it has the ability to change a whole school's approach to INSET. Thus, it is the duty of course organisers to ensure that this element is given an even higher profile in the taught course for the course participants. It is important to remember that most of the course participants are inexperienced INSET providers. Perhaps a larger amount of time could be spent studying the important elements of in-service training in the first term and in ensuring, perhaps in supervision time, that any school-based meetings are carefully planned. School-based meetings could then be held in the second term of the taught course, with the support of the LEA tutor if required.

The above study appears to justify the course initiative for attempting to develop the whole school approach through the school-based project. It is now the responsibility of course providers to ensure that course participants receive optimum levels of knowledge and help in this area to ensure success in all the participating schools.

References

Alexander, R. (1980), 'The evaluation of inservice courses for teachers, the challenge to providers', *British Journal of Teacher Education*, 6 (3).

Ambrose, I. (1987), 'National initiatives in special education training: intention and impact', in T. Bowers (ed.), *Special Educational Needs and Human Resource Management*, (Beckenham: Croom Helm).

Bolam, R. (1982), *School Focussed In-Service Training*, (London: Heinemann).

Elliott, J. (1978), *The Classroom Action Research Network Newsletter*, (Cambridge Institute of Education).

Eraut, M. (1983), 'What is learned in in-service education and how?' *British Journal of In-service Education*, 9 (1).

Fullan, M. (1982), *The Meaning of Educational Change* (New York: Teachers' College Press).

Harnett, P. (1986), 'A new approach to INSET for special needs: the Bedford course for special needs coordinators', *British Journal of In-service Education*, 13 (1).

Henderson, E. and Perry, G. (1981), *Change and Development in Schools* (Maidenhead: McGraw-Hill).

Iano, R. (1986), 'The study and development of teaching: with implications for the advancement of special education', *Remedial and Special Education*, 7 (5).

Keast, D. (1982), 'School-based in-service and the providers', *British Journal of In-Service Education*, 9 (1).

Kerry, T. (1985), 'Barriers to, and pre-conditions for, innovation in primary teaching', *British Journal of In-Service Education*, 12 (1).

Moses, D. Hegarty, S. and Jowett, S. (1987), 'Meeting special educational needs: support for the ordinary school', *Educational Research*, 29 (2).

Powers, D. (1983), 'Mainstreaming and the in-service education of teachers', *Exceptional Children*, 49 (5).

Sebba J. and Robson, C. (1987), 'Short school focused INSET courses in special educational needs', *Research Papers in Education*, 2 (1).

CHAPTER 4

Keeping in Touch with Reality: the Role of a Special Needs Coordinator in a Secondary School

Steve Cooke

'What does a Special Needs Coordinator actually do?' – a question often on the lips of those with a hazy recollection of the remedial teacher, housed in a store cupboard and armed with a mysterious battery of tests, charts and a name for every type of learning deficiency. This case study looks at my role as a coordinator/head of special educational needs (SEN) in a mainstream secondary school over the second half of a school year.

The context

The school is a single-sex, 11–18 comprehensive with a population of approximately 600 boys (1988) and a staff of 40 teachers. With the possible exception of a small number of students who have a hearing loss, there has not been any major change in the intake of students with special educational needs as a result of the move to integration brought about by the Warnock Report (1978) and the 1981 Education Act. However, within the last ten years, special educational needs provision within the school has developed away from being an 'ambulance service' whereby the remedial department, consisting of one teacher with an allocation of ten periods, withdrew a few small groups in order to help them overcome literacy difficulties.

The present provision of the special educational needs department consists of a mixture of withdrawal (to a large central special educational needs resource base) and support across the curriculum within mainstream classes, the vast majority of which are banded/setted. This provision is in keeping with the slow move of many mainstream educational establishments towards a 'whole school' approach. The change has been made largely in response to the prevailing view among educationalists that a child's failure to adapt to the expectations of a school is in fact a failure of the school itself in determining its provision.

During the last five years, the SEN department has worked with some 15–30 per cent of the pupil population annually, although it is very unlikely to be working with 30 per cent in any one week. The department has great flexibility afforded by the fact that its members can arrange their own timetable with very little restriction. (For example, in the school year 1987–8, only two of the possible 52 special educational needs staff periods were fixed by the school timetabler – the other 50 periods could be used as the special educational needs department desired.) To maintain such a high degree of control over what it does, the department must be able to show that it makes good use of its freedom of timetabling in order to justify this degree of flexibility in future – particularly in the light of an imminent amalgamation, falling rolls, staff cutbacks and demands for staff time by new initiatives such as TVEI (Technical and Vocational Education Initiative), GCSE and HAP (Hertfordshire Achievement Project).

Since being appointed, first as head of the remedial department, then as head of special educational needs and more recently as coordinator of special educational needs, I have been allowed considerable freedom to develop the role in consultation with colleagues. However, there has never been a written job description. Although I embarked on the Advanced Diploma course partly for my own satisfaction and professional development, I also wanted the school to benefit directly by the 'use' of course assignments to help carry out a major review of special educational needs provision within the school and of my role in particular. This review was initiated in the autumn of 1986.

My long study was to be an analysis and criticism of my own role. I chose a period of 19 weeks from February to July 1988 and documented all my school-related activities during that time. One of the objects of the exercise was to identify the main areas in my role as a special educational needs coordinator within the school and to analyse the amount of time spent on each area. I wanted to avoid preconceptions, so I needed to gather data and allow patterns to emerge gradually (in the manner suggested by Glaser and Strauss, 1967), rather than trying to identify role areas first and then fit the data into these.

Methodology

In carrying out this investigation, I followed Hopkins' (1985) four stages of classroom research, i.e.

(1)   data collection
(2)   validation
(3)   interpretation
(4)   action.

Data collection

My main method of collecting data for this study was through the process of self-shadowing – a form of participant observation – supported by numerous brief informal interviews with staff and students.

The most important task initially was to devise a way of keeping a 'time diary' – an accurate, continuous record of activities, but one that would not, either by the time it required, or by its intrusion into dealings with students and staff, affect the nature of those activities. I rejected pen and paper methods as cumbersome and time-consuming, and retrospective recording as potentially distorted. Instead, I decided on using a micro-cassette recorder and transferring records to a database on my home computer. This had the advantages of being very quick, and of allowing me to record observations without having to classify them at the time by filling in a table or checklist. The micro-cassette recorder was familiar to many students, not only as they had already seen it in use during the previous year as an aid to record keeping, profiling and so on, but also from a trial run that I instigated for one week during the half-term prior to the investigation proper.

The transfer of data from cassette to computer proved to be very time-consuming and tedious, involving the playback of short sections followed by frenetic typing of information before I forgot it and had to replay the section of tape. However, the database proved very useful as it allowed me to create a table starting with just a few columns – detailing date, place, duration to the nearest five minutes and a description of the activity – and then to add further columns as I later attempted to group together and classify data (see Table 4.1).

Table 4.1 Time diary – an example of the original data

Time	Place	Sub	MA	WD	Comments
35	S	E	2	03E	SEN Admin: preparing statement for DD + K3
90	S	E	N	03E	Staff badminton
90	H		2	03F	Video copying/planning + looking through papers
60	S	E	N	03F	Basketball practice – 1st year
120	S	E	2	03F	Basketball practice + Saturday club
45	S	E	N	03F	Newspapers
75	H		N	03F	Marking/recording/planning English – 3J
75	H		N	03G	Reference for SVS
150	H		N	03G	Cricket Admin – NHSS leagues
5	H		N	04A	Setting video
25	S	E	N	04A	Newspapers
40	S	E	2	04A	Planning Maths – 1.4 + K3
25	S	F	N	04A	Cricket Admin – NHSS leagues
70	S	L	2	04A	Newpapers + individual work (TAF absent)
20	S	F	N	04A	Planning Maths – 1.4 in computer centre
70	S	L	N	04A	Maths – 1.4 in computer centre
30	S	F	2	04A	English + K3
70	S	L	N	04A	Maths – HAP
15	S	F	N	04A	General Admin
35	S	L	N	04A	Cricket Admin – school (LH absent)
35	S	L	N	04A	English – 1st years
80	S	E	N	04A	Academic Board
105	H		N	04A	Long study – setting up database
10	H		N	04A	Reference for SVS
120	H		N	04A	SEN Admin: preparing statement for DM
100	H		N	04A	SEN Admin: preparing SIR for DR/JSY
5	H		N	04B	Setting video
15	S	E	N	04B	Newspapers
15	S	E	N	04B	Planning English – 2D
5	S	E	N	04B	Planning History – 2D
40	S	E	2	04B	Planning English – 2D + K3
25	S	F	N	04B	Liaising with ESL teacher RE. work for MV
35	S	L	N	04B	English – 2D
35	S	L	N	04B	History – 2D
20	S	F	2	04B	Planning Maths – HAP + K3
70	S	L	2	04B	Maths – HAP + preparing HAP records/profiles – maths
20	S	F	2	04B	DM + K3
30	S	F	N	04B	Yr. Heads meeting
35	S	L	N	04B	English – 1D
35	S	L	N	04B	English – 2D
15	S	F	N	04B	Planning English – 1B and 1D
35	S	L	N	04B	English – 1B
35	S	L	N	04B	English – 1D
95	S	E	N	04B	Basketball practice – 1st year
150	S	E	N	04B	Parents meeting – 3rd year options

See key overleaf

Key:

Time	=	length of time (in minutes) spent on activity
Place	=	S (School), H (Home), O (Other)
Sub	=	L (Lesson time), E (Extra time), F (Free time)
MA	=	multiple activity: N (No), 2 (two activities)
WD	=	week (01-19) and day (A-G)
		(03E would be Friday of the third week)
Comments	=	notes about the actual event

K3	=	supervising pupils in resource room
NHSS	=	North Herts Secondary Schools
Academic Board	=	school management group
SIR	=	Schools Internal Record
ESL teacher	=	support teacher for bilingual pupils
HAP	=	Hertfordshire Achievement Project
2D, 1.4, etc	=	student groups
DD, DM	=	initials of individual pupils

For the purpose of possible analysis and reporting, activities were recorded as having occurred in one of three main places: school (S); home (H); other (O).

● The time at school was conceived as consisting of three main subsections:

(i) Lesson (L-time) – that part of school hours normally assigned to teaching periods.

(ii) Free (F-time) – breaks and lunch period, which are nominally the teacher's own time, but during which he/she may engage in teaching activities. I also included in this section, rather than in L-time, registration and assembly times, as I did not have the responsibilities of a form to deal with at these times.

(iii) Extra (E-time) – all the time outside school hours.

● The time at home had no subdivisions.

● 'Other' was subdivided into:

(i) Cambridge Institute of Education (C).

(ii) Teachers' Centre (T).

At the end of 19 weeks I had an extensive database of over 1500 separate records or timed events. This was far too unwieldy to analyse but by changing the date data from weeks and days to half-termly categories and by combining records that were identical in all aspects apart from the length of time (see Table 4.2), I was able to reduce the number of records in the database to 321, which was far more manageable. I nevertheless took the precaution of keeping a print-out and a disk copy of the original information.

Table 4.2 Percentage of each time period spent on the main categories

Time period	(Mins.)	Percentage of time period spent on:						
		M	P	L	A	S	D	R
Whole time	(77,315)	3.5	13.5	7.8	4.9	48.5	11.8	9.8
Half-term: 1	(20,280)	8.5	10.5	7.1	8.4	41.4	15.2	8.9
2	(26,975)	2.1	16.9	6.9	3.7	46.2	16.0	8.1
3	(30,060)	1.9	12.3	9.5	3.7	55.1	5.8	11.8
School: L-time	(20,780)	0.9	0.1	2.5	0.5	89.8	5.3	1.0
F-time	(8,995)	12.3	3.8	28.4	0.3	30.8	18.1	6.2
E-time	(16,850)	5.3		11.9	1.0	61.9	12.9	7.2
Place: School	(46,625)	5.4	0.8	12.5	0.8	63.0	12.4	5.2
Home	(18,830)	1.9	30.7	1.2	17.4	3.8	18.0	27.1
Other	(11,860)		35.8	1.5		62.7		

Key:
M = management   L-time = lesson time
P = professional development   F-time = free time
L = liaison   E-time = extra time
A = assessment
S = student contact
D = preparation and development
R = resource base management

Note: Figures in brackets show the total number of minutes spent on each time period – e.g. events recorded throughout the 19 weeks of the investigation totalled 77,315 minutes (or 1,289 hours to the nearest whole hour).

Validation

Critics of participant observation studies are very concerned about the validity of the data. Cohen and Manion (1985) point to the lack of precise quantifiable measures that are the hallmark of survey research and experimentation. As Table 4.2 shows, I did in fact collect a great deal of quantifiable data. Hook (1981) points to the problems caused by the participant observer's duality of roles, in that the teacher cannot separate him or herself from the teaching task with all the concomitant demands of the school situation. This poses problems of achieving objectivity.

I would argue that I overcame these problems in the following ways:

(a) By using simple, easily managed procedures (a personal dictating machine and self-shadowing) that minimised distortion of the 'normal' school day.

(b) By asking the opinions of other staff and/or students when I was analysing data that could be interpreted in a variety of ways. For example, in a lesson where I was not the only teacher present, was the subject teacher (S) leading the lesson; was I, the researcher (R), taking a leading role and allowing the subject teacher to act as the support teacher; or were we taking an equal responsibility (E) for the lesson? By gathering accounts of the teaching situation from three quite different viewpoints – those of the co-teacher, the students and the participant observer – I attempted to validate my observations and interpretations through the process of triangulation in the manner suggested by Glaser and Strauss (1967) and explained by Elliott (1976–7).

(c) Through the process of 'saturation' (or 'snowball sampling'), in the manner suggested by Becker (1958). As I developed my categories from observation of my coordinator's role (because of the extent of my original data), I was able to test the data repeatedly against these categories in an attempt to modify or falsify the category.

These processes ensured that the results had 'internal validity' – i.e. they described what was really happening in this situation.

I was not particularly concerned about the 'external validity' – generalisability to other situations – of my results. When I started this study, my main purpose was to bring about improvement of practice within the school where the research took place. I always expected the results to be situation and context specific.

Interpretation of results

Having produced the list of activities, I then attempted to identify the purpose of each activity and to look for similarities. By this process of 'progressive focusing' to develop categories – becoming more directed, systematic and selective – not only was I able to make the data more manageable, but I was also able to develop a 'grounded theory' (Glaser and Strauss, 1967). This is so called because the categories developed are 'grounded in' (i.e. originate from) the data gathered in and applicable to a specific social situation.

During this process, a number of events proved difficult to code and it was at this stage that important decisions had to be made on the following problems:

● How to record periods of time where I appeared to be doing a number of different jobs within the same time period;
● How to categorise a week-long field trip;

Table 4.3 My roles as SEN coordinator

---

(1) *Management* [3.7%]
   (a) Acting as part of school management system - consists mainly of attendance at formal meetings (55%)
   (b) Links with governing body - keeping governors informed of SEN provision within the school (45%)

(2) *Professional development* [13.5%]
   (a) Externally - includes everything related to Advanced Diploma course: meetings of Stevenage area SEN coordinators organised by SEN adviser (97%)
   (b) Internally - Baker Day (3%)

(3) *Liaison* [7.8%]
   (a) With external agencies - educational psychologist, ESL teacher, HAP maths moderator, SEN adviser (14%)
   (b) With members of the school staff - academic, pastoral, social and informal staff development (74%)
   (c) With parents - academic, pastoral, reviewing Statements/SIR documents (12%)

(4) *Assessment* [4.9%]
   (a) Record keeping - Statements, SIR documents, other records (50%)
   (b) Marking tests - administering standardised tests (13%)
   (c) Report writing (16%)
   (d) Profiling - HAP maths (21%)

(5) *Student contact* [48.5%]
   (a) Teaching by self (27%) - class teaching (68%)
                             - withdrawal (28%)
                             - extra, occurs outside lesson time (4%)
   (b) Team teaching (30%) - subject teacher leads lesson (20%)
                           - equal responsibility for lesson (68%)
                           - support teacher leads lesson (12%)
   (c) Field trip (21%)
   (d) Voluntary (22%) - sport (64%)
                       - Saturday Club, youth-type club (3%)
                       - organising waste newspaper collection (15%)
                       - supervising students in SEN resource base outside lesson time (18%)

(6) *Preparation and development* [11.8%]
   Consists of marking, recording and planning work

(7) *Resource base management* [9.8%]
   (a) Reviewing materials (29%)
   (b) Planning materials for others (33%)
   (c) Cataloguing resources (11%)
   (d) General administration - filing papers, locating resources, tidying up after lessons, etc. (27%)

Key:
Figures in square brackets = % of total time spent on role
Figures in round brackets = % of role time spent on activity

● Whether or not to include a variety of activities that at first glance appeared irrelevant to my role as special educational needs coordinator;
● How to subdivide the major category of 'Preparation and Development'.

Once these decisions had been made and having coded and validated the data through the processes described, I developed a model for describing my actual role as special educational needs coordinator over the period of a term and a half (see Table 4.3). For easy reference these data are summarised in diagrammatical form in Figure 4.1.

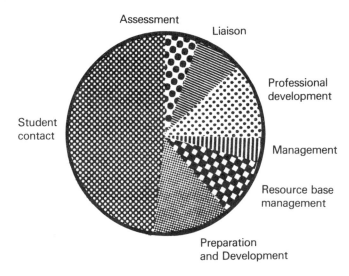

Figure 4.1 Percentage of whole time spent on my seven role areas

Action

Having created some meaning out of the evidence, it is then necessary to build on these conclusions in order to plan realistic strategies. If such developments are likely to affect other staff, then it is essential that those staff are involved in the changes – they need to be given the opportunity to study the research findings and to argue for alterations in the proposals. In other words, they need to share in the ownership of any changes that may affect them (Lieberman, 1986; Hopkins, 1986).

What did I learn?

Having obtained an analysis of time spent on various role areas from the database, I attempted a critical evaluation of my role in the light of suggestions from current literature.

My analysis would confirm that student contact has been a priority, especially during lesson time (89.8 per cent of lesson time and 48.5 per cent of total time). I would defend this on the grounds that, to be successful with students, a teacher must develop a good working relationship, and this requires time. This is particularly true of students who lack confidence or who have a record of failure in one or more important skills/curriculum areas. It is, therefore, important that the special educational needs coordinator establishes a good relationship early in a student's school career, maintains this relationship throughout the first year, and then ensures consistency of approach from one year to the next.

I have found that involvement in extra-curricular activities, seeing students in a variety of different classroom settings, using the process of negotiation, using collaborative learning and involvement in field trips (which have a strong social emphasis) can all help to establish the type of trusting relationship with students that is necessary if one is to be successful in meeting their special educational needs. It must be remembered that features of a good school go beyond the classroom. The special educational needs coordinator has an important part to play in ensuring the preservation of each student's 'dignity' (Hargreaves, 1982). On the whole, this can be achieved by an accessible and appropriate curriculum, and it must not be forgotten that the 'hidden' curriculum is often a most influential factor for many students with special educational needs.

Some would argue that far more time should have been spent on other role areas, such as management, professional development of other staff, liaison and resource base management, in order to develop a 'whole school' approach to special educational needs. As Bowers (1987b) suggests: 'It is quite apparent that we are seeing a movement away from special needs specialists working directly with children' (p. 98). However, it must not be forgotten that most teachers would like to concentrate on teaching and keep other elements of the job to a minimum if they could.

I believe that a 'whole school' policy is necessary and that it is essential to involve far more of the human resources already available to the school other than the special educational needs specialists. I would argue, therefore, that not only can some aspects of the 'newer' role areas be carried out through the 'changed' student contact role of the special educational needs coordinator, but that this is a more efficient, successful and enjoyable way of developing a 'whole school' approach to special educational needs.

If other people apart from special educational needs teachers are to contribute to a 'whole school' provision, then the special educational needs coordinator will need to develop a variety of relationships with others – staff, parents, other pupils and representatives of external agencies. In my view, the most successful ways of achieving worthwhile relationships with other staff are:

● Establishing classroom credibility – being prepared to take whole classes, just like 'ordinary' teachers, being prepared to deal with difficult groups/individuals, and being prepared to teach lessons while the subject teacher takes a subsidiary role – in other words, doing what most teachers regard as the basic function of the profession: teaching students.

● Liaising with them (5.8 per cent of total time), particularly over cooperative arrangements, but also over anything related to special educational needs, including the planning of future lessons, reviewing previous lessons, pastoral matters (for both individual pupils and groups), INSET, and advising staff or listening to staff. Also it may help if teachers can meet socially at functions such as an after-school badminton club.

● Being concerned with the 'whole school' and not just matters relating specifically to special educational needs. In fact, I strongly believe that I am a school teacher first and a coordinator of special educational needs second. The special educational needs coordinator's involvement in organising voluntary activities has untold benefits for the standing of the special educational needs department in the eyes of the staff, for it is seen to be contributing to the whole school and I would argue, therefore, that the whole school is far more likely to be prepared to contribute something to the provision of special educational needs as a result.

When a reasonably trusting and open relationship has been built with another staff member, it is very unusual for that person to be reluctant to share their classroom. Once it has been agreed to enter into a cooperative teaching arrangement, it is important that some form of contract is drawn up and that time is put aside for planning and evaluation (both formative and summative), otherwise, as Thomas (1988) points out, the initiative: 'may not simply disintegrate; its debris may act as a barrier to further development, or to innovation in other areas, long after the event' (p. 151).

Effective two-way staff development – ensuring that the subject teachers feel that they own any changes that are occurring – can then take place in the classroom at the same time as teaching and also when liaising. In addition, students are not suffering because their subject teacher is on 'yet another INSET course'.

Thus, by building up relationships both with students and teachers, the special educational needs coordinator can gradually develop 'whole school' provision for special educational needs.

Flexibility of provision

Secondary schools are notorious for their very rigid structures. In meeting special educational needs, we have to work for a flexible and informed system of support that is open to constant reappraisal and change, that can respond quickly to emergencies but also respond in a stimulating way to long-term needs. For this reason any one style of provision or any static remedy is likely to be inadequate. The greater the responsibility the special educational needs coordinator has for establishing his/her own timetable, the more room there will be for flexibility in the school's provision.

Table 4.3 shows the variety of special educational needs provision during lesson time, including teaching of small special sets, withdrawal for learning and/or behavioural difficulties, and support teaching. I was involved in teaching/supporting whole classes in the following curricular areas: English (for 31% of the time), Maths (30%), PE (15%), Information Technology (6%), Geography (6%), History (6%), Science (3%) and Social Education (3%).

The role of support teacher is very much a developing one. There are still many problems connected with the role:

- ○ Not all teachers are happy having a second teacher in the classroom.
- ○ There is insufficient time for proper liaison, without additional staffing being available.
- ○ There are occasions in a team teaching situation when two teachers are not needed in the class. On such occasions, the teachers concerned must be prepared to recognise this fact and come to an agreement that one of the teachers – not necessarily the support teacher — uses his/her valuable time more profitably.
- ○ Support teachers should not interfere in an insensitive way, especially where considerable progress is already being made through the efforts of the subject teacher.
- ○ There are – very occasionally, fortunately – times when support teacher and subject teacher fail to form a working relationship.

○ The skills one requires as a support teacher are very different from the skills of the traditional remedial teacher. Some teachers find it very difficult to modify their child-related skills to the new people-oriented management skills of the consultative role.

○ I would agree with Rouse (1987) who found that, if support staff were not involved in sharing activities such as preparation, presentation, marking, report writing and attending parents' evenings, then this could lead to feelings of resentment on the part of the subject teachers and boredom by support teachers as a result of 'role underload'.

○ I personally received considerable motivation from being completely responsible for one class in a particular subject. As a full-time support teacher, I would have missed out on this.

Nevertheless, support teaching has also produced considerable benefits. For example:

○ The special educational needs teacher is serving in a preventative capacity rather than picking up the pieces in crisis intervention.

○ When combined with a structured liaison procedure, support teaching can be the most powerful form of school-based INSET, if not all INSET.

○ Support teaching often results in staff looking at the appropriateness of the curriculum not just at the deficits of the students, which a withdrawal system tends to encourage.

○ Support teaching reduces pressure on the subject teacher, especially where difficult classes are involved.

○ Team teaching encourages group work, which in turn encourages students to work collaboratively, supporting one another and seeking solutions to the problems presented by their tasks and activities.

○ Support teaching can also overcome problems of labelling through social and academic integration; give special educational needs students access to the specialist knowledge of the subject teacher; help with the problem of 'pacing' a lesson for a class containing students with a wide range of ability; and alleviate the problem of scarce teacher time.

○ I also noticed the unexpected benefits from co-teaching arrangements discovered by Rouse (1987) in his school: more practical science taking place; subject teachers preparing better lessons; greater continuity in the case of staff absence; a decrease in the number of sanctions used by some teachers; special educational needs teachers seeing some of their students against a different educational backcloth.

Special educational needs resource base

Another important feature of my school's special educational needs provision in recent years has been the establishment of a central resource base. This has brought about a number of benefits (many of them unexpected), and I feel that to have such a central resource base from which a special educational needs coordinator can reach out in order to support both teachers and students is an essential characteristic of special educational needs provision. Advantages afforded by the use of the central resource base included the following:

(a) Before and after school and at break and lunchtimes the base could be used by any student within the school – not just students with special educational needs. This reduced the possibility of any stigma being attached to it. During these break and lunchtime sessions, peer tutoring on a very informal basis developed and some students often helped with some of the simple but time-consuming tasks in the special educational needs coordinator's general administrative role.

(b) Having a large room meant that classes to be team taught could be brought to the support teacher rather than the support teacher taking materials and himself to another room. Again, this reduced the possibility of any stigma being attached to the room. Having experienced the resource base in a team teaching situation, a number of staff and/or classes preferred to continue making use of the base when I had stopped supporting that group. Teachers coming to the room with classes or when seeking advice could see examples of work achieved by other groups or might see alternative forms of learning/teaching/grouping styles in action, after which they might try similar ideas themselves.

(c) Having a large room also permitted flexible groupings and more readily allowed situations whereby teaching of one class at the same time as withdrawal of individuals or small groups from another class could be attempted.

An important practical point is that such a resource base should include a telephone to enable the special educational needs coordinator to carry out his/her liaison role with parents and external agencies with a minimum of time wasting.

Reflections

As well as bringing to the fore these vital features of special educational needs provision – good relationships through a high level of contact, maximum flexibility and a central resource base – this investigation also pointed to a number of shortcomings that future action needs to rectify.

Special educational needs support group

We need to resurrect in the school the special educational needs support/curriculum group, consisting of key/link teachers from each curriculum area. Dates should be arranged for regular meetings to be held throughout the year. One of the most important jobs of this group will be to evaluate the appropriateness of the curriculum for students with special educational needs, remembering to include student opinion in the process. The results of such an evaluation should be passed on to the management team with suggestions for action. If strengths and weaknesses of the curriculum are not identified, there are dangers of: an inappropriate, modified curriculum lacking balance; disaffection and disruption during students' time at school; and poor preparation for when the student leaves school.

Although evaluation of the curriculum did take place during the investigation, I have not singled out this role in my model as a separate category – a possible weakness of the model.

Professional development

I felt that, in the short term, too high a proportion of my time (13.5 per cent of total time) was spent on personal professional development. However, I did find a huge advantage in being able to relate this to the practical work situation. Virtually every moment spent on personal professional development was designed to be of benefit not only to me but, even more so, to the school. I found this to be probably the best feature of the Advanced Diploma course design and the fact that it was a part-time course taking place in the middle of a normal teaching week meant that theory could be easily and readily applied. Provided that the school reaps benefit from my involvement in the Advanced Diploma course, then this short-term imbalance would be justifiable on long-term grounds. Therefore, in addition to informal, internal INSET, mechanisms do need to be set up to ensure that research and knowledge pertaining to special educational needs can be distributed in a more formal way. I would suggest:

● a special educational needs noticeboard in the staffroom;
● inclusion of appropriate material in the weekly Staff Bulletin;

● the creation of a small staff library, which would include a selection of books covering special educational needs.

Initiating staff development programmes does not appear as a separate function. I am strongly against such programmes when they take place during time that would normally be spent teaching in the classroom and there is an adverse effect on the students who miss out on 'normal' teaching. Now is not the correct time to start a major initiative of this sort, particularly in my school. The reasons for this are many:

(1)   There has been enormous pressure for change in schools in the last few years and many pupils have suffered when staff have been out of school on training programmes. Many staff are 'shell-shocked' by the degree and the rate of change – a period of consolidation is needed in many schools, yet the Education Reform Act (1988) will bring about more changes and put increased demands on all teachers. In addition, my school will be going through an amalgamation process throughout the coming years.

(2)   One must balance the needs of the special educational needs department with those of the whole school and I would suggest that other areas are in greater need of staff development. A number of staff have already participated in special educational needs development programmes during the last three years.

(3)   There is increasing evidence within the school that teachers consider the least effective form of INSET to be the formal lecture, but they value workshops on materials and in-class support from specialist teachers.

(4)   It must not be forgotten throughout that staff, myself included, are very wary of innovators:

Over the years, more experienced teachers have been cajoled into various forms of curricular and organisational innovation. They will be aware of the 'band wagon' phenomenon whereby 'innovators' have moved on to higher realms in education, leaving their less fortunate colleagues to unravel and solve the problems which are left in their wake. The apparent 'negativism' of long-serving teachers should not always be interpreted as opposition *per se* but, rather, as a wary suspicion of the motives of the latest 'innovator'. (Wynn-Jones, 1987, p. 200)

I would argue very strongly that, in the climate of never-ending change, the doubters should not be ignored.

All the above leads me to believe that INSET should normally occur within the school itself and should be on a small scale, at least until the unfair demands now being placed on teachers are considerably reduced. I would claim that such staff development in the area of special educational needs is already occurring – a claim that appears to be backed up by comments made during informal interviews with staff. This is being achieved through supporting teachers in the class-room and through informal, individual or small group discussions, which are part of my liaison role.

Continuance of traditional roles

The more traditional roles of the remedial teacher must not be forgotten completely. For example, I would argue that the assessment role continues to be an important one. For me, assessment consists of two essential components: identification – a screening process through which students with special educational needs at a specific time are identified; and diagnosis – the process that investigates in detail the needs of each identified student. Without a good assessment process, students with learning difficulties are unlikely to achieve their full potential, because it would be very difficult to plan efficient special educational needs provision.

Effective use of time

Despite the use of time-shifting – trying to ensure that certain duties do not impinge on lesson time – I do need to make a more efficient use of time in many ways and to encourage other staff to do the same. Four particular areas would be:

○ Marking – I would like to see far more instances of students marking their own work.

○ Preparation of materials for one-off lessons or courses – should be kept to a minimum. Successful materials, adapted if necessary, should be used with other classes in the same year and/or in future years.

○ Peer tutoring (Topping, 1988) and collaborative learning (Brandes and Ginnis, 1986) – once organised, these can release valuable time to the teacher.

○ The effective use of parents resulting from good home–school links. As was the case with staff liaison, the great majority of parental liaison took place outside lesson time. If it is part of the special educational needs coordinator's role to liaise with parents, especially if it is in order to promote programmes of parental help, then time is a very important factor.

As Sigston (1987) points out: 'parental involvement projects raise key management issues in relation to the introduction of institutional change and person management . . . . The full adoption of new practices therefore requires decisions about the redistribution of resources' (pp. 136-9).

Will the special educational needs coordinator receive time in lieu for those evenings spent meeting parents or will extra staff be appointed so that this development can proceed? The latter is unlikely; the former is a possibility; but will the special educational needs coordinator be able to find other tasks that he/she can give up? When considering the alternatives, the research indicating the long-term effectiveness (or ineffectiveness) of withdrawal-type programmes (Collins, 1961 and 1972; Newcomer and Hammill, 1975; Johnson and Pearson, 1975), especially when compared with recent research findings showing the effectiveness of parental support programmes (Tizard, Schofield and Hewison, 1982; Topping and Wolfendale, 1985), needs to be considered. However, if parental support programmes and peer tutoring are to work successfully, time must be spent on liaising with the tutors.

Conclusion

Bowers (1987a) calls for considerably more job analysis in order to give 'an accurate picture of the real requirements of many special needs posts rather than a distanced view of what they ought to entail' (p. 13). I have attempted such an analysis but any reader trying to draw conclusions from this investigation should bear in mind that the role outlined is:

- *Time-specific*. The role is a developing one that is constantly changing. I might well have obtained very different results if I had carried out the same study throughout the first, rather than the second, half of the year. This study is an amalgam of everything I covered over a period of 19 weeks. Special educational needs coordinators cannot be 'super-teachers' who can do everything and give all responsibilities equal priority. It is necessary to change emphasis from day to day, from week to week, from term to term, and from year to year. The coordinator must be realistic about the role; a process of job analysis, producing a clear role perception followed by forward planning, should help prevent high levels of adverse stress.
- *Context-specific*. Because each coordinator works in a school that is a unique educational setting, it is impossible to draw up a single nation-wide model for the role of special educational needs coordinator. Just

as the coordinator assesses the needs of students before drawing up programmes for them, so he/she must assess the needs of the whole school and gradually develop a role that will best meet those needs.

Acknowledgements

I would like to thank the course members for the contribution to my role model; the course tutors for their support; the staff and pupils at school; and my wife, Julia Cooke, for all her help.

References

Becker, H. (1958), 'Problems of inference and proof in participant observation', *American Sociological Review*, **28**, December, 652–60.
Bowers, T. (1987a), 'Human resources and special needs: some key issues', in T. Bowers (ed.), *Special Educational Needs and Human Resource Management* (Beckenham: Croom Helm).
Bowers, T. (1987b), 'Internal and external support: roles and definitions', in T. Bowers (ed.), *Special Educational Needs and Human Resource Management* (Beckenham: Croom Helm).
Brandes, D. and Ginnis, P. (1986), *A Guide to Student-Centred Learning* (Oxford: Blackwell).
Cohen, L. and Manion, L. (1985), *Research Methods in Education* (London: Croom Helm).
Collins, J. (1961), 'The effects of remedial education', *Birmingham University Institute of Education: Education Monographs*, No. 4 (Edinburgh: Oliver & Boyd).
Collins, J. (1972), 'The remedial reading hoax', *Remedial Education*, **7**(3), 9–10.
Elliott, J. (1976–7), 'Developing hypotheses about classrooms from teachers' practical constructs', *Interchange*, **7**(2), 2–22.
Glaser, B. and Strauss, A. (1967), *The Discovery of Grounded Theory* (Chicago: Aldine).
Hargreaves, D. (1982), *The Challenge for the Comprehensive School: Culture, Curriculum and Community* (London: Routledge & Kegan Paul).
Hook, C. (1981), *Studying Classrooms* (Victoria: Deakin University Press).
Hopkins, D. (1985), *A Teacher's Guide to Classroom Research* (Milton Keynes: Open University Press).
Hopkins, D. (1986), 'The change process and leadership in schools', *School Organisation*, **6**(1), 81–100.
Johnson, D. and Pearson, P. (1975), 'Skills management systems: a critique', *Reading Teacher*, **28**, 757–65.
Lieberman, A. (1986), 'Collaborative research: working with, not working on', *Educational Leadership*, **43**, 28–32.
Newcomer, P. and Hammill, D. (1975) 'ITPA and academic achievement', *Reading Teacher*, **28**, 731–42.

Rouse, M. (1987), 'Bringing the Special Needs Department out of the cupboard', in T. Bowers (ed.), *Special Educational Needs and Human Resources Management* (Beckenham: Croom Helm).

Sigston, A. (1987), 'Investing in successful parental partnership', in T. Bowers (ed.), *Special Educational Needs and Human Resource Management* (Beckenham: Croom Helm).

Thomas, G. (1988), 'Planning for support in the mainstream', in G. Thomas and A. Feiler (eds), *Planning for Special Needs: A whole school approach* (Oxford: Basil Blackwell).

Tizard, J., Schofield, W. and Hewison, J. (1982), 'Collaboration between teachers and parents in assisting childrens' reading', *British Journal of Educational Psychology*, **52**, pp. 1–15.

Topping, K. (1988) *The Peer Tutoring Handbook: Promoting Cooperative Learning* (London: Croom Helm).

Topping, K. and Wolfendale, S. (1985), *Parental Involvement in Children's Reading*, (London: Croom Helm).

Wynn-Jones, P. (1987), 'The teacher as manager', in M. Hinson (ed.), *Teachers and Special Educational Needs* (Harlow: Longman).

CHAPTER 5

Pupil Reactions to a Differentiated Curriculum

Susan Marsh

> *Scene*: The staff room of a secondary school.
> *Time*: The present.
> *Characters*: Teacher 1, studying the day's cover notice. Other teachers talking, marking, reading the *Times Educational Supplement*.
>
> *Teacher 1*: I see Fred's off on TVEI INSET again.
> *Teacher 2*: No problem, it's all GRIST so we'll have a supply in.
> *Teacher 1*: Well, he's down for 4Z PSE, so I'd better keep an eye on them. I wonder what they've done in IEA.
> *Teacher 2*: Not much. They're mostly HAP types aren't they, not GCSE kids?

To a teacher in one of today's comprehensive schools this scene is very familiar. The issues it raises, though by no means new, particularly reflect the developments in secondary education over recent years.

- First, and most obviously, the language has a mystique that excludes outsiders, and an outsider in this context can also be a pupil. What does the pupil – or parent or employer – make of the acronyms PSE and IEA or even the full titles 'personal and social education' and 'industrial and econcomic awareness'.
- Secondly, in order to keep teachers informed of recent initiatives there are frequent in-service training courses (INSET)
- Thirdly, teachers are willing to take on extra responsibility to ensure the smooth running of the school, but often they do not know what takes place in lessons run by their colleagues.

● Fourthly, there is a divide between the so-called 'academic' and 'non-academic' pupils: a divide that is seen to exist in behaviour and worth as well as in intellectual ability.

As a support teacher for special needs in a comprehensive school, I am particularly concerned by this last issue. Comprehensive schools have assimilated two traditions: one is derived from the grammar school and is dominated by the requirements of external examinations; and the other is derived from the secondary modern school with its curriculum loosely based on the teachers' perceptions of pupil needs (see Holt, 1978). The school in which I teach tries to reconcile these two traditions in the 4th and 5th years by offering a substantial compulsory core together with a wide choice of subjects within option groups. In this way we hope to provide a broad and balanced curriculum for all pupils, while allowing for individual differences in ability and interest.

During the past three years we have implemented a number of new curriculum initiatives including:

the Technical and Vocational Education Initiative (TVEI).
the General Certificate of Secondary Education (GCSE).
the Hertfordshire Achievement Project (HAP).

I recently carried out some research to study how these initiatives are intended to accommodate the needs of low attainers and how they affect the classroom experiences of these pupils. In this chapter I shall be describing how I planned my research and what I learnt from it. In particular I shall refer to comments made by low-attaining pupils that indicate their perception of the curriculum.

Research

A written prescription of what is intended should happen in schools, (Stenhouse, 1975, p. 2)
All the opportunities for learning provided by a school. (DES, 1980, p. 1)

These two definitions of curriculum reflect Stake's distinction (1967) between the 'intended' curriculum and the 'observed' curriculum and it was under these headings that my research was planned.

The intended curriculum

First, I studied the aims of those initiatives that had been introduced in

54

the school and tried to establish what common approaches were suggested. This was done in the following stages:

Stage 1 – Reading the literature

- syllabus, criteria, analyses of the initiatives
- evaluation of pilot projects
- guidelines for curriculum development

Stage 2 – Discussion

- teachers involved in implementing the initiatives
- outside agencies, e.g. Director of HAP, County Advisor for Curriculum and Methodology
- pupils in the process of making their option choices for the 4th years.

The observed curriculum

Next I observed what actually took place in the classroom. Three 4th year pupils, who over the years had all received help from the special needs department agreed to my shadowing them and I was able to attend all except one of the subjects on their timetables on several occasions. Thus my research involved two further stages:

Stage 3 – Observation

- classroom observations of three 4th year low-attaining pupils
- brief interviews with the pupils after each lesson
- brief interviews with the teachers after each lesson

Stage 4 – Interviews

- formal interviews with pupils using photographs as a stimulus
- formal interviews with teachers using photographs as a stimulus.

Methods

In order to reduce the mass of information that I gathered about the intended curriculum to manageable proportions, I kept in mind two questions:

What are we trying to do?
How are we trying to do it?

These led me to try and identify the aims and approaches that seem common to the different initiatives. Finally I drew up the following list, which I used to guide my observations.

The aims and approaches suggested under TVEI, GCSE and HAP include:

- an emphasis on what the pupil knows, understands and can do;
- the encouragement of self-esteem by giving the pupil more responsibility;
- the involvement of pupils in self-assessment that is both formative and summative;
- the establishment of clearly understood short-term as well as long-term goals;
- the development of thinking skills through research and problem-solving;
- a teaching situation that makes use of practical work and active participation by the pupils;
- group work, which shows an ability to work cooperatively and to communicate with others;
- the encouragement of oral expression through discussion and explanation;
- the use of tape, video, computer/word-processor, etc., particularly as an alternative means of recording;
- an insistence on the relevance of the work undertaken to the pupil's present and future life;
- a close link with industry.

Whilst observing lessons I made written notes in the form of a field diary. As these notes were largely descriptive, I felt the need for a systematic record. I therefore made an engagement schedule for one lesson on each of the subjects followed by the three 4th year pupils. I recorded how the pupils were occupied at 5 minute intervals and related this to classroom activities. During each lesson I also took a series of photographs, which I used later as a reminder for myself, but more particularly as a stimulus for interviews. I always respected the wishes of those who asked not to appear in the picture and, in fact, one of my three subjects only appears with her back to the camera. Most of the photographs are also being used for purposes outside my study, e.g, display, recording in HAP subjects.

Many staff room conversations about the curriculum were spontaneous and I felt it would be restricting to take notes. I tried to follow up the discussions later when I interviewed teachers in a more formal way and was able to write down my notes. Most interviews, both with staff and pupils, were 'semi-structured', by which I mean that I used a series of pre-planned questions that I could expand if I felt the need. Where I needed a quick opinion from pupils, e.g. during a lesson, I took notes, but during the longer interviews with them I used a tape recorder. A year ago when I wished to record pupils on tape, they were concerned that I was 'collecting evidence' about them for use in the school. This year there was an easy familiarity with the machine, arising, I was told, from the fact that tape-recorders are frequently used in English, modern languages and most HAP subjects.

Some methodological issues

In carrying out research, it is important to establish the validity, reliability and confidentiality of the information gathered.

> *Validity* is establishing that what is actually recorded and analysed matches what the researcher claims to record and analyse. I hoped to affirm the validity of my information by viewing it from different standpoints. The criteria for TVEI, GCSE and HAP are set out in published papers. A further view of these initiatives as they have been put into practice is given by evaluation documents, especially in areas where there have been pilot project, (e.g. Wallace, 1985; Hutchinson, 1985). In addition, some of the teachers in the school explained what they thought the initiatives had to offer in their subject.
>
> I also used this form of 'triangulation' when observing lessons. I recorded views from three different sources – the pupils, the teacher, and myself as observer.
>
> *Reliability* is ensuring that what is observed on one day can be replicated in similar situations in the future. I observed as many lessons as possible given my own teaching commitments. I then showed my recordings to the teachers and pupils and asked whether this was a 'typical' sample of lesson activity. On three occasions an engagement schedule was repeated for a pupil who believed that the first one was not a fair record. Because I was unable to observe sufficient of the PSE lessons to make my analysis reliable, I omitted this subject entirely from my study.
>
> *Confidentiality.* I discussed my plans with the teachers and pupils whose lessons I wished to attend. I explained that any information they gave me was confidential and I would only quote from it with their permission. In fact permission was always granted, and on one or two occasions opinions were held so strongly about aspects of the initiatives (e.g. lack of coordination in the timing of different INSET courses) that I was particularly asked to include them in my study.

We are told that when God made time, He made plenty of it, but this is rarely the experience of teachers. Carrying out research while teaching is a time-consuming occupation, but it has encouraged me to stand back from my classroom role and consider what we are doing. The study I made was only possible with the cooperation and forbearance of very busy fellow staff and I have been fortunate that my colleagues are so supportive.

The intended curriculum

The Technical and Vocational Education Initiative (TVEI) was implemented in the school in 1986 and now involves every pupil in the 4th and 5th years. Breadth and balance in the curriculum are encouraged by the existence of a core curriculum (English, mathematics, science, personal and social education) and three option groups, from which each pupil must choose one subject – Group 1: 'hard technology', e.g. craft, design and technology; Group 2: 'soft' technology, e.g. food industries; Group 3: aesthetic and creative, e.g. music, fashion and textiles. Pupils must also choose two subjects from Group 4, which is headed Humanities but in fact offers a wide selection of subjects, e.g. child care and extra science.

In this way every pupil now follows the same curricular structure, but within the option groups there is a choice of subjects. In the first year of TVEI (1986–7) pupils were given a free choice of subjects within the groups, but not all courses were felt to be appropriate for the low-attaining pupil. In the following year more HAP (Hertfordshire Achievement Project) courses were introduced and some pupils were encouraged to select these instead of existing GCSE courses. Thus, under the umbrella of TVEI, there is a variety of provision, which lays itself open to the charge of divisiveness.

The revised edition of the Herts TVEI Extension Handbook (HCC, 1988) claims that the authority's policy is that 'schools should attempt to eliminate unjustified curricular differentiation' (Appendix 1, para 2.10). Later on, it states that 'All students are entitled to learning experiences which are suitably differentiated according to individual need' (Appendix 4, para 2.2).

Is this the contradiction that it first appears? I feel we have to examine *what* we are intending to provide for our low-attaining pupils. If we are offering a different curriculum from that offered to other pupils, then we are restricting the experiences that we provide. If, however, we are offering different approaches that we feel will take note of their individual needs then we may well broaden the range of

58

experiences. The danger lies in making premature assumptions about the capabilities of the pupils.

The introduction of General Certificate of Secondary Education courses in 1986 was an attempt to replace the former divisive system, in which some pupils (the top 20 per cent) studied for the General Certificate of Education and some (the next 40 per cent) for the Certificate of Secondary Education. Sir Keith Joseph, then Secretary of State for Education, claimed that the aim was to bring 80–90 per cent of all children up to the average level of CSE Grade 4. It is intended that the GCSE will be appropriate for a wide range of pupils because it will enable the pupil to demonstrate what he or she 'knows, understands and can do' (GCSE General Criteria, para. 16).

However, GCSE requires differentiated assessment. For many subjects pupils are still selected according to their perceived ability and entered for different papers. The examinations are supposed to record what a pupil achieves, but I doubt whether someone awarded a Grade F (F for failure?) will feel a sense of achievement.

The Hertfordshire Achievement Project has been developed for those pupils, who, it is felt, will not be able to show what they know and understand in a GCSE examination. One of HAP's strengths is that it is devised by those responsible for implementing it. Practising teachers suggest courses to meet the needs of their low-attaining pupils. They draft objectives and then pilot the schemes. The course content is not prescribed. Individual schools devise a scheme of work that allows the pupils to fulfil the objectives, and progress is recorded on a profile and negotiated with the pupil.

There is no doubt in my mind that HAP occupies a lower status than GCSE.

'When you take an HAP certificate in for a job, other people walk in with O levels and they think "She ain't that clever".'
(5th year pupil)
'But this HAP certificate won't help him get a proper job.'
(Parent)

Hutchinson (1985), in his early evaluation of HAP, notes that headmasters do not publicise the course for fear of cultivating the public image of a school that caters for those with learning difficulties and thereby deterring the more able pupil.

In my interviews with subject teachers I asked, 'Do you think that there should be a separate HAP group for your subject?'

'Yes. In a combined group there is too much writing for HAP pupils and not enough for GCSE.' (English)

'Yes. When the two groups were combined, I did not get the friendly, supportive atmosphere I get now. I should like to see a HAP group which is a single unit for all subjects.' (Science)

'Not really. Information Technology is taught in a small group on an individual basis anyway.' (IT)

'No. I think as many pupils as possible should take GCSE because it has a higher standing with employers.' (Child care)

'Yes. I want to give them something useful they can enjoy at school without the pressure of working for an exam.' (Fashion and textiles)

Before considering in more detail what the pupils think about a differentiated curriculum I should like to emphasise that pupils may follow a mixture of HAP and GCSE courses. As many as 12 take only one HAP subject and only three pupils do not follow any GCSE courses at all, so there is a variation which allows pupils to work to different levels in different subjects. Nevertheless we must ask ourselves if we are perpetuating a system where pupils can say:

'I do GCSE CDT. They do HAP, 'cos they're thickies.'

(4th year pupil)

The observed curriculum

I observed the lessons followed by three low-attaining pupils in the 4th year whom I have named Sheila, Alan and Brian. Sheila follows four GCSE courses and four HAP courses. Alan follows one GCSE course and seven HAP ones, and Brian follows two GCSE courses and six HAP ones. All three told me that they had chosen the subjects by themselves, although Sheila had discussed her career prospects with her mother.

I circulated a questionnaire to the 3rd year pupils who had just made their option choices, to study how children came to their decisions. The options had been explained by the teachers, but most children reached a decision with the help of their parents (76 per cent). The two most common reasons given for their choice were that the subjects would be useful for a career (80 per cent) and that the pupils enjoyed them (63 per cent). Only 43.5 per cent said they were good at them. Most pupils agreed that mathematics (80 per cent) and English (77 per cent) should form part of the core curriculum, but only 49 per cent wanted to include science. Pupils commented that limitations on their

60

choice were made by the groupings, but within each group they could choose what they liked.

Between them Sheila, Alan and Brian follow GCSE courses in design and communication, art, food industries, child care, information technology and rural studies. All these subjects are concerned with the development of practical skills. Often it is assumed that low-attainers are only interested in practical work, and this is given as the reason for not developing thinking skills.

I asked the pupils what sort of work they preferred.

> 'I like working with my hands.' (Alan)
> 'I like practical work, not writing and discussion all the time.' (Brian)
> 'I don't like having to sit down and work in silence.' (Sheila)

These opinions were confirmed by what I observed and by the way the engagement schedules matched the lesson activity. Alan described it as 'learning to think on the job'. Interestingly, Alan who chose only one GCSE subject, commented:

> 'I'm a slow writer, I'm a slow reader, I can't spell, so I can't handle the GCSE courses.'

Clearly he associates GCSE courses with predominantly written work. The GCSE course he has chosen is information technology, which involves all the activities he mentions, but in a form in which, it was clear to me, he felt comfortable.

One of the complaints voiced most frequently by the pupils is that there is more theory than they had expected in the subjects chosen:

> 'The trouble with home economics, now we're doing it as GCSE food industries – you're doing more writing than what you are cooking.' (Sheila)

Teachers commented that the work of these three pupils is below the standard of other pupils. They require extra support or they become discouraged. I noticed Sheila copying from another girl's work in design and communication. She told me she usually did this as she finds the subject more difficult than she had anticipated. Brian, however, commented:

> 'The subjects are harder than I thought they'd be, but I like what I've taken up.'

When given the extra support, the pupils' work showed visible evidence of success. In rural studies, the vegetable plots, which require long-term attention from Brian, do not receive it and produce only a small crop. In his cold frame, where results are produced more quickly, he grows some very healthy lettuces and radishes. Alan's final versions on the computer show signs of adventurous thinking and, once the mistakes are corrected and erased, they can be forgotten.

Sheila, Alan and Brian followed HAP courses in community studies, fashion and textiles, child care, instrumental enrichment, craft, design and technology, and the core subjects of mathematics, English and science. Some of these were chosen by the pupils for the content of what they offered. Community studies may combine elements of history, geography and social studies, but it has no direct counterpart among the GCSE subjects and therefore no comparison. Fashion and textiles is, with child care, part of home economics, but has developed far from the traditional needlework, making an appeal to boys as well as girls.

> 'We learn all sorts of extra things. That bit where we were doing colour and we learnt about wiring, that'll be useful when I'm a mechanic.' (Alan)

Instrumental enrichment is a thinking skills programme that has been used with academic 6th formers, but is normally used with low-attainers. Certain pupils are encouraged to choose it, but because other pupils do not understand what it is about, very little comment is passed.

> 'I didn't choose it. I got told to do it, but it's all right 'cos I'm learning things, you know, talking in a group and working things out together.' (Richard, another 4th year pupil)

Problems in self-esteem seem to arise where a direct comparison can be made between GCSE subjects and HAP ones, e.g. CDT and the core subjects. Pupils enjoyed the methods used in HAP CDT and Science.

> 'In HAP, group work is essential and it is assessed, but in GCSE even if pupils work cooperatively, they are assessed independently.' (Mr Taylor, science)

> 'We all chip in with ideas about how we could do the project and we decide on the best way.' (Alan, HAP CDT)

The teachers involved in these subjects commented that the pupils would not be able to cope with the theoretical concepts necessary for the GCSE and the calculations and written recording. In the HAP lessons that I observed some of these difficulties were by-passed by using aids such as computers and calculators.

English and mathematics are seen to be important by the pupils, even though they clearly associated them with areas of failure in their own lives.

> 'You should do mainly reading and writing in English even if it is boring, because if you can't write you can't fill in an application form and if you can't read, you still can't fill it in.' (Alan)

As these subjects are part of the core curriculum they are compulsory and this I feel adds to the lack of motivation from the pupils. There is also a history of failure. These are not subjects they have chosen on the basis of enjoyment. The teachers try to make the topics relevant to the pupils' lives, but the pupils suspect that the basic intention is to practise mathematics and English skills. They see this as sugar-coating the pill and the sugar soon wears off.

What do the pupils feel is important if a subject is to be worth while? Two ideas in particular came out in the course of my interviews.

- Firstly, the pupils need to feel that they are being valued as people, and this will be shown by the way they are treated.

  > 'He knows he can trust us, right? He can leave us to get on and we won't muck about.' (Brian)

  > 'I like him better than all the other teachers. He treats you like an adult not like a kid.' (Alan)

  > 'When I came back here [from a college course] I thought "My God, they're treating us like little children".' (Sheila)

- Secondly, pupils need to feel that the subject is 'real' – that it has a value in their world.

  > 'RE, you just sit and listen, same with social studies and health education. They're just there to fill up the timetable.' (Sheila, on Personal and Social Education)

  > 'At college, you worked in the kitchen with other people until you got the job done. Here they put you in lessons and when the bell goes, you go to another lesson.' (Brian, after a catering course)

I asked the three pupils whether they felt that doing HAP was a good idea. Sheila strongly opposed the idea of having to do GCSE in subjects she found difficult. A recent experience when all the 4th year took the same English examination had embarrassed and angered her.

'I was still reading the questions and the girl next to me had written two pages, it was, well, embarrassing. She must think I'm thick or something – They made me look a right idiot in that exam.'

The two boys were evidently happy with most of the HAP courses, if not with other people's reactions to them.

'This is much better than last year 'cos you've got HAP. It's much easier, well not easier, more straightforward.' (Brian)

'Well, of course, other people call you "thicko", but it's really boring if you don't understand what's going on. What I think is, all courses should be like HAP, not having GCSE, but everyone do HAP. They'd like it much better.' (Alan)

Conclusion

Alan's suggestion is worth considering. GCSE was intended to cater for pupils across the ability range, but it still has a built-in system of differentiation to allow for the use of a written examination. HAP courses lead to a record of achievement including a negotiated profile that is filled in as different skills are mastered. Pupils are not expected to reach the same standard at the same time. Perhaps we should ask ourselves if examinations are essential to 16+ assessment. David Hargreaves, quoted in the *Times Educational Supplement* (1988), predicts an end to the 16+ examination with the rise of modular studies and graded assessment. Nevertheless the place of the 16+ test is reaffirmed by the National Curriculum, which makes very little reference to low-attainers, other than to say that they can be withdrawn from testing altogether. This is an extreme form of differentiation.

Sheila, Alan and Brian appear to enjoy lessons where they are given the opportunity to play an active role. This may involve increased responsibility in planning their own activities, working cooperatively with others and discussing with the teacher the assessment of their work. What they claim to dislike is being set apart from their peers because of the way the subject is to be examined.

Fred and his colleagues from the staff room scene with which I began, together with all of us who have a concern for low-attaining pupils, need to find out what recent initiatives in secondary education have to offer us. We should do away with mystique of the language and make it plain that what is important is what is taught rather than what is tested. If the curriculum is not to be dominated by a new

64

examination system that differentiates between pupils and in the old way equates worth with ability, we shall have to develop a method of recording progress other than by examination certificate. I believe we should look to Records of Achievement. These could take the best from approaches suggested under TVEI, GCSE and HAP, ensuring that the National Curriculum tests fulfil their true purposes as guides to progress rather than goals in themselves.

My study reports some of the pupils's reactions to a differentiated curriculum. It is easier to point out the problems than to find a solution, but I have argued that we should make the most of the approaches put forward by recent education initiatives and develop the use of Records of Achievement. The approaches will vary according to the lesson activity and the participants. The Records will contain different details about different pupils. What should remain the same is the importance that we attach to the individual needs of all our pupils.

References

DES (1980), *A View of the Curriculum* (London: HMSO).
Hargreaves, D. (1988), in Nash, I. 'Imminent end of 16-plus exam foretold', *Times Educational Supplement*, 25 March 1988.
HCC (1988), *Herts TVEI Extension Handbook* (revised).
Holt, M. (1978), *The Common Curriculum – Its Structure and Style in the Comprehensive School* (London: Routledge & Kegan Paul).
Hutchinson, B. (1985), 'The public image of HAP', Interim Report No. 3 (unpublished paper).
Stake, R. (1967), 'The countenance of educational evaluation', *Teachers' College Record*, **68**(7), 523-40.
Stenhouse, L. (1975), *An Introduction to Curriculum Research and Development* (London: Heinemann).
Wallace, R. G. (1985), *Introducing Technical and Vocational Education* (Basingstoke: Macmillan).

CHAPTER 6

Providing Curriculum Access

Geraldine Callaghan

The Warnock Report (DES, 1978) and the 1981 Education Act (ACE, 1983) advocated the right of pupils with special educational needs to have access to the curriculum experienced by all pupils. The implication of this has undoubtedly contributed to the changing size and composition of the special education population. This change is apparent in my own school, which caters for pupils experiencing moderate learning difficulties, where referrals during the past four years have been dramatically reduced. The evidence indicates that an increasing number of pupils with special educational needs are receiving their education in mainstream schools alongside Warnock's 18 per cent.

My original research question arose from a desire to address this particular concern; that is, how the ordinary secondary 'school provides pupils with special educational needs access to the curriculum experienced by all pupils. I selected a local comprehensive school in which to conduct my research. I am grateful for their full cooperation and support.

The school advocated a 'whole school' approach to the support and development of pupils with special educational needs. 1st years were taught in mixed-ability groupings and all followed a common core curriculum (Hargreaves, 1984). The special needs department time-table support of its 1st year pupils across the year group, placing an emphasis in the humanities lessons – 20 per cent of the timetable was allocated to the teaching of humanities.

Originally, I fully expected that the course of my investigation into pupil access to the curriculum would lead me to consider the following:

○ the role of the support teacher within the classroom;
○ modifications of the delivery/content of the curriculum.

However, initial observations and discussions revealed that these factors were to have a reduced impact in terms of enabling pupil access. Subsequently these issues proved insignificant to the outcome of this study. Access to the curriculum was to remain the definite responsibility of the subject teachers. Consequently the study was an attempt to examine a group of pupils in their classroom context. In particular it examined the question:

> How can classroom teachers enable pupils with special educational needs to have access to the curriculum?

The study was my attempt to evaluate and examine this concern. My aim was to highlight issues that need to be focused on to enable teachers to become more effective in planning and meeting the special educational needs of all the pupils they teach.

Research methodology

This section outlines the techniques used to gather information during the research process. It also includes comment on the problems I encountered.

The head of special needs selected a 1st year class containing several pupils who experienced learning difficulties. During my classroom observations I identified five of these pupils; the head of department and class teacher confirmed these findings. None of these pupils' educational needs was maintained by a Statement.

The intention of the study was to investigate a group of pupils in their natural classroom environment. After examining possible research methods for collecting the data, I decided on a naturalistic research approach (Lincoln and Guba, 1985). This enabled me to employ a combination of different methods of collecting information. In the naturalistic approach, the theory develops from the research and is concerned with describing and interpreting situations. In this type of research the teacher's perspective is central, permitting me to define the problem as I viewed it. I believed my study fitted firmly into this framework.

Data collection

The data were gathered during nine visits to the school, by means of the following:

(1)   observations within the classroom;
(2)   interviews to determine the teacher's viewpoint;
(3)   interviews to determine the pupils' viewpoint;
(4)   developing theory grounded in the data (Lofland, 1976, in Allen, 1986).

The observations took the form of a narrative approach (Hook, 1981). This technique is less structured and offered a more flexible observational technique appropriate to the reporting of classroom analysis and practice.

Initially the classroom observations I recorded were very general. The observation schedule was divided into three columns, allowing the recording of observations, the time the observation occurred and my interpretation of the observations. Two days were spent following the class to all lessons and recording their experiences. These observations yielded a vast amount of information. In commencing the process of analysing the data, certain issues recurred and appeared to have significant connections with pupil access to the learning experience. A further day's observation of the class was administered, focusing more exclusively on the themes generating from the data. This included a more detailed examination of the pupil-teacher interactions.

From the observations, an extensive list of themes was recorded. This was reduced by careful processing through the material. Common issues emerged and these were combined further. A final selection was based on how frequently a theme was reinforced. The search through the data enabled certain issues to be eliminated whilst establishing relationships between others (see Table 6.1). The reviewing of the material confirmed that these issues were grounded in the data. The final reduction produced five key issues, all concerned with the management of learning experiences.

These issues formed the basis of my interviews with the pupils and teachers. The style employed was the focused interview technique (Hook, 1981).

Number of interviews	*Type of interview*
5 pupils (3 girls, 2 boys)	group
5 teachers (English, maths,	individual
art, humanities, special needs)	

I interviewed the pupils as a group, hoping this would increase their

68

Table 6.1 Reduction of the data

Themes	Five key issues
Feedback to pupils on their work Use of praise by the teacher Feedback session at the end of lesson Teacher talks but does not ask the pupils questions	Feedback
Interaction – pupil/teacher, teacher/pupil, pupil/pupil Strategies employed by children to learn Asking other pupils to help How does teacher involve pupils in lesson? When does the teacher teach? Where does teacher direct the lesson from? Can children talk, or do they work in silence? Is the lesson delivered by the teacher to the whole class?	Pupil learning styles
Has the pupil enough information to carry out the task? The teacher's responsibility to provide a stimulating session Children should be certain of the task How the teacher uses instructions to aid pupil understanding Teacher talks but does not ask the pupils questions Where does the teacher direct the lesson from?	Presentation of instruction
Establishing method of interaction with teacher Pupils to get to know teacher expectations for classroom Responsibility of pupils to organise equipment quickly Resources available to children How is the room arranged for working?	Physical learning environment
Teacher to direct pupils whilst they are working Movement by teacher to see all the pupils Drawing pupils attention back to the task Should the teacher be certain of what the children have learnt during the session? Teacher talks but does not ask questions	Monitoring

confidence, encourage them to relax and provide them with time to think. They did not appear to be unduly influenced by other group members, but offered a varying perspective. However, five pupils in a group aided by a fairly lengthy interview schedule resulted in an unnecessarily long interview. The topic guidelines employed with the teachers enabled good coverage of all the relevant issues raised through the observations.

Confidentiality was guaranteed to both pupils and teachers. This was notably an important issue for the teachers. Gaining their confidence enabled them to respond freely and openly to the interview questions, overcoming possible reservations about who might have access to the interview material. Tape recording all interviews enabled me to focus my full attention on the interviewee, but resulted in an enormous number of words to be transcribed.

With the gathering of new observational and interview data, existing ideas were challenged and re-formed. The theory of the study developed. This was based on the issues raised and their importance if effective access to learning was to occur for pupils with special educational needs.

Problems of the research design

I have outlined the techniques I used as the researcher. There are, however, practicalities associated with conducting any research and a number of difficulties and issues that regularly confront the researcher. Giving consideration to these problems and developing an awareness of the limitations formed an integral part of my experience of the research process.

An immediate criticism of my naturalistic research design could be the tendency to make subjective interpretations. Yet the naturalistic method recognises the presence of the researcher. Validation of this type of research was also problematic. With this in mind I decided to certify my findings through the use of 'triangulation' (Cohen and Manion, 1985). Triangulation is a process that allows the various points of view of those involved in the investigation to be presented – in this case, my own, the teachers' and the pupils'. Each of these differing perceptions would have an essential contribution to the findings of the research and could confirm the researcher's observations and interpretations.

The time involved in conducting a naturalistic enquiry, researching in an unknown environment and interacting with the different individuals and classrooms did prove to be a real constraint on what could be achieved in a given time. Moreover, 15 hours of observation produced a large amount of data for analysis, with emerging issues calling for further research.

I admit the analysis of the data was both the most critical and the most painful period of the research process. There were occasions when I wished I had set out to prove a predetermined hypothesis! As an inquiry, working with the material afforded opportunities for creativity, particularly in attempting to analyse and make sense of the numerous connections. I experienced moments of panic about whether I was capable of perceiving the connections and associations from amongst the data. Could I provide explanations for my findings?

Could I see further ways forward? These occasions called for me to draw on my perseverance, sense of humour and tutor support.

Following this was the move from data analysis to presentation. What theory would I present?

Looking back, I believe I have gained enormously from undertaking a naturalistic inquiry employing qualitative research methods. I believe I have experienced a unique opportunity of studying life in a classroom, observing with an open mind the teaching and learning environment and the interactions of the people working within it. Despite these implied constraints, I feel the data collected from both observations and interviews proved to be both explicit and meaningful.

The findings

The theory arising from the data implies that there are five key issues to be considered in providing access for children with special educational needs to the learning provided in the ordinary classroom. It also suggests that the ordinary classroom teacher's level of awareness must be raised to assist them to be more effective in meeting the needs of all their pupils. I have grouped these five issues under the general theme 'Managing the Learning Experience'. They are:

(1) the physical learning environment
(2) the styles of learning
(3) the presentation of instructions
(4) the feedback of pupils
(5) the monitoring of pupil progress.

The inquiry has attempted to evaluate the importance of these factors in determining curricular access. I will now consider each of them in a little more detail.

The physical learning environment

Each classroom presented itself as a unique environment where pupils interacted with quite different sets of routines and teacher expectations. These differences were quite marked and the onus to learn to adapt was unquestionably placed on the pupil.

A teacher interviewed about the ways pupils were encouraged to seek help offered the following view:

'If there are too many children waiting then I insist they sit down, they will have to wait for attention. There are some children who draw attention more than others, and they are probably the ones who need it less than the others who make less effort.'

This teacher operates this system aware that it fails to serve all the children. It was conspicuous how a teacher's role became less dominant in the classroom as s/he became less mobile. Even when a teacher remained at the front of the class employing a more formal procedure of raising hands, this was not always effective in improving the situation, for the pupil with special educational needs often remained obscure, rarely asking questions. The principal means of contacting the teacher was for pupils to leave their places, often leading to a disrupted working atmosphere. The varying situations confronting the pupils and their ability to manage the differing teacher demands have definite implications for the view pupils have of the organisation and atmosphere of their learning environment.

Equally, pupils met diversity in the availability and distribution of resource materials. Teachers universally agreed that pupils should be given unlimited, independent access to the equipment they needed. However, in practice there was no uniformity of approach – each teacher established their own method. The results varied in the different classes. Pupils were seen organising themselves quickly and efficiently in certain situations, yet in others it led to chaos and unnecessary time-wasting.

The final point relates to the grouping of children within the classrooms. Some teachers did not attach any importance to the grouping of pupils. In contrast, others attached enormous significance to the room arrangement and what this communicated to the children about their learning environment. The English teacher expressed her view:

'We've got tables, so now I can group them anyway I like. It's important . . . they see the set-up of the room as part of the learning situation.'

Another teacher confirmed the importance of pupils liking the atmosphere, especially the arrangement of the room, believing a classroom arrangement could be a very daunting experience for some pupils:

'Great long lines of pristine desks and chairs and neat little bits here and there.'

The majority of teachers did not exploit the possibility that varied groupings could offer different pupils in assisting cooperation and working towards supporting their social, emotional and academic needs.

Presentation of instructions

The inquiry highlighted this as a key area in relation to pupil access to the learning. Undoubtedly, it is the intention of every teacher to provide pupils with a learning experience during the lesson. Therefore, the elected mode of presentation, if appropriate, could facilitate understanding and effectively meet the differing pupil needs. Teacher talk appeared to be a vitally important link in the introduction of a task. Generally, however, pupils in the study felt their teacher spoke too frequently.

'He talked too much' . . . 'when Mr X keeps talking it's rather boring 'cos we're trying to get on with our work' . . . 'at the end when he was talking we hadn't finished' . . . 'we didn't listen' . . . 'I was trying to catch up'.

The children appeared unaware that teacher talk might directly relate to the task they were engaged in. This suggests a need to employ a variety of methods of presentation, to include visual, demonstration and the direct involvement of the pupils.

Teachers' use of language emerged as another possible inhibitor of understanding. One teacher confirmed the need for different presentations for the 'higher academics' than for the 'lower academics'. Yet, no obvious intervention was apparent during the 1st year maths lesson to ensure that the pupils understood the mathematical language used in the booklets.

Observed lessons frequently lacked introductions and pupils were not informed of the task or its purpose. I noted lessons where pupils were instructed to take out a particular book and the session commenced irrespective of the readiness of the group. The children seemed fairly well acquainted with this style of working, whereas I felt lost. Equally impressive was the high level of motivation displayed by the pupils and their ability to remain on task, even when they experienced hostile working conditions. In contrast to this, other lessons exhibited pupils paying attention, instructions being clearly delivered and varied presentation. Prominent in classrooms where instructions to pupils were unclear or inadequate was a follow-up period of questioning the teacher or each other. Given that questioning could be a fairly crucial technique of gauging pupil understanding, this type of pupil–teacher interaction was all too absent before the commencement of a task. The pupils confirm:

'. . . the teacher he don't explain it very good, he gets the hump . . . more time to explain.'

'... I don't get the words, if the teacher could help me and explain the words.'

'I didn't understand the words what we had to fill in, I did ask my partner to explain it and I went up to Sir ... we asked each other ... I did understand a bit ...'

This suggests pupils have not gained sufficient understanding to commence the task independently. No strategy was implemented to check their knowledge of the task.

In trying to assess the subject teachers' awareness of teaching pupils with special needs, I inquired whether they consciously employed different strategies with these pupils:

'I'm not aware that I do, I think that's one area where I'm perhaps at fault.'

'I take too much for granted ...'

'It doesn't occur to me that children of that age can't read a worksheet, it really doesn't.'

The pupils gave their opinions about a worksheet they had used in a previous lesson:

'Some of the words were hard to read ...'

'... some of it didn't make a bit of sense if you didn't know a certain word.'

'Some words were really hard ... like ... "immigrant".'

This demonstrates the mis-match between the reading demands of the task and the actual reading ability of the pupils.

An interviewed teacher valued the use of oral work to involve children of all abilities and to maintain interest. However, her colleague was adamant that creating a remedial group was by far the best method of coping with pupil differences.

Employing different media could assist in the presentation of instructions. Yet teachers continued to use the blackboard or, alternatively, employed well-designed worksheets that were accompanied by little or no explanation. My findings indicated that pupils were relying on passively listening to teacher talk, copying down notes or struggling to read information from worksheets pitched at an inappropriate level. One pupil summed up how she would like the lesson to be achieved:

'Discussion at the beginning, then work, then have another discussion at the end before the bell, so we can fully understand it.'

Learning styles

The evidence strongly indicates that the style of learning endorsed by teachers has a critical impact on the effectiveness of learning situations. Consequently teachers need to focus on the significance of the interactions operating within the classroom environment that can assist more effective pupil access.

The teacher-directed approach was the most prominent learning style. This was characterised by a whole class method of instruction, generally leading to pupils working individually on their tasks. A teacher who rarely insisted on silence in his lessons recognised that there were a large number of children requiring help. He perceived himself and other pupils as a possible source of assistance. Yet, even within this framework, pupils with special educational needs still presented a problem, particularly those who elected to sit and work alone. These pupils were observed opting out of group discussions or from working with a friend. Subsequently they experienced difficulties relating to their learning and their ability to complete the task. One pupil admitted:

> 'I got a bit bored of it today and I kept rushing up to L and telling her jokes...I couldn't put enough effort in...I didn't finish the task...they were hard, I just left it...I'll do it the next lesson.'

The situation suggests that the teacher should adopt a strategy more specifically aimed at creating a more supportive learning environment. Working with a partner could promote increased on-task behaviour and lead to greater motivation. A structured cooperative learning style that fosters the skills of collaboration and working alongside others (Madden and Slavin, 1983; Johnson and Johnson, 1983) could make a positive contribution to the quality of the pupils' learning experiences and reduce the tendency to 'opt out'.

When questioned about their learning, pupils indicated a preference to have opportunities to discuss and talk about their work; to be actively involved; to make their own contributions; and to be valued. Lessons where talk was not encouraged tended to confine pupils within a solitary environment. Teachers should be alerted to the fact that an individualised framework without any flexibility, together with work inappropriately matched to pupil needs, could be a recipe for disaster.

To counter pupil talk from being incidental and seldom related to the task, it is important for teachers to structure groups that emphasise talk as part of the learning process.

Interviewed teachers advocated the following as being effective if pupils were to have a chance to access the intended learning:

○ breaking down tasks into smaller units – a task presented in its entirety may be too complex;
○ an emphasis on practical-based experiences;
○ a reduction in the demand for written work;
○ pupils working together.

This implies teachers working towards improving the quality of their pupils' learning. But they are surrounded by colleagues who fail to recognise the role of the pupil in the learning situation. Observations exposed lessons that demanded little or no verbal input from the children, where they were given insufficient opportunity to question and too few occasions to interact with the teacher. With respect to pupils with special educational needs being enabled access to learning, teachers need to reorganise their classrooms and be prepared to accommodate a variety of learning styles, to ensure pupil involvement and to maximise the opportunities for learning at all levels.

Feedback

Feedback is a means of checking on pupil understanding. It could be highly beneficial at the instructional phase of the lesson, through the use of questioning. A teacher making effective use of this technique was observed selecting pupils at random to answer questions. This is a valuable process in reinforcing correct responses, rectifying wrong ones and gauging the pupils' understanding of the task.

The principal feedback to pupils from the teacher occurs during the task or, more commonly, at its completion. All interviewed teachers unanimously agreed that feedback is absolutely vital, particularly with the weaker child. One teacher offered the following insight:

'. . . it needs some sort of feedback continually through the lesson to keep them motivated. Perhaps if they don't get it that's when we reach situations where they don't finish pieces of work, they begin to struggle.'

The emerging pattern from his own and other classes clearly showed pupils initiating the feedback. These were frequently the brighter, more extrovert children, who were willing to approach the teacher and show their work. Undoubtedly this reinforces the importance of teachers leaving their desks after the instruction period to take responsibility for initiating the interaction with their pupils. This could assist pupils to remain seated and positively reinforce on-task behaviour.

The data revealed that teachers who do not impose their own system become directed by the pupils, with the special educational needs pupil so often absent from these interactions. Despite the teachers' earlier support for feedback, it was noticeable how many remained at their desks or moved at the pupils' request only. In certain classes, involvement with pupils was used solely for the purpose of marking, as opposed to a contact time for a teaching/learning experience.

I asked pupils how they knew they were doing their work correctly:

'We don't really know . . . when we've filled it in and tried to get it correct we go to sir.'

'After I've finished working I go up to sir and ask if he could mark it, he says he hasn't got time, so we don't bother now.'

These pupils were not receiving comments from the teacher during the process. Their work was marked at the end of a session, probably in their absence. Where work does not include a feedback remark, understanding and motivation for the task could be totally devalued. Much of the work seen simply registered a mark.

Praise was valued highly and believed to contribute directly to positive gains for pupils in the areas of confidence and encouragement. This was particularly true for pupils with special needs, who require enormous amounts of praise and feedback during phases of new learning.

It is essential for teachers to recognise that the quality of guidance and interactions they provide for their pupils are directly linked to the achievement of learning outcomes.

Monitoring pupil progress

Recording what pupils achieve enables their progress to be accurately monitored and provides information about the success of the teaching in meeting pupil learning needs. The recorded information could be developed into an ongoing pupil record.

In general, the school's view of monitoring progress relates to information yielded through tests and exams. Within the classroom setting, this is represented as marks registered for particular pieces of work. An over-reliance on this system could reinforce a sense of failure for some pupils, leading eventually to demotivation and possible disaffection. Therefore, a shift in emphasis by teachers and a matching of appropriate tasks/pupils is needed.

Teachers in the study indicated that they monitored their pupils' work by marking completed assignments. An interviewed teacher doubted the value of looking along a line of marks to attain an accurate picture of a child's progress or ability. On the other hand, she valued marking work purely against the pupil's own performance to measure individual progress. This enabled pupils of differing abilities to attain similar marks. The English teacher's system of recording consisted mainly of comments based on individual pupil strengths and weaknesses. These teachers' views highlight the discrepancies they experience when working in an exam-oriented secondary school system. They favoured and supported the differing needs of the pupils found within mixed-ability groupings. Yet there was no indication of a system developed to record the pupils' progress in this way.

The observations revealed an absence of the type of monitoring that occurs when teachers talk to pupils as they carry out set tasks, or on its completion. Also, little attention appeared to be directed towards setting time limits, or stating what pupils were aiming to achieve during a lesson. It was noticeable that incomplete assignments frequently became a pupil's homework. This could have a negative effect and discourage pupils from attempting to accomplish set tasks within an allocated time. Pupils definitely need to aim for realistic targets set at appropriate levels.

Amongst pupils with special needs there emerged a persisting theme of pupils not completing work; tests not attempted; hands never raised to answer questions; and teachers never approached for help. Alongside these pupils were teachers who at times appeared painfully unaware of their pupils' predicaments. Numerous other interactions and incidents constantly demanded their attention.

Research evidence supports establishing key concepts or objectives relating to a lesson or series of lessons, which could be developed into an ongoing pupil record (e.g. Rosenshine, 1983). The record could inform about the content of a lesson, skills to be mastered and include pupil/teacher comments. Chiefly, it would aim to record the achievements of the pupils. It would also provide a means of self-evaluation for the teacher.

Conclusion

The intention of the study was certainly not to criticise teachers. Rather it was to highlight issues to do with teaching pupils with special needs within the classroom. It seems to me that the effective classroom characteristics raised by the study are fundamental in enabling access to the curriculum for pupils with special educational needs. Consequently they provide a useful agenda that individual teachers might use to review their own practice.

One of the aims of the study was to investigate a specific environment, with the chosen research design supporting this inquiry approach. The research findings thus closely relate to the organisation and ethos of this setting, and have a particular value within this context.

Undoubtedly, the intention of research is to inform. In accordance with this I have made available and distributed the findings of this study to interested parties (including an offer to the school to disseminate the issues of the study through an INSET programme). Certainly the research has implications for the school at the centre of the study. At an organisational level, the development of self-evaluative methods based on my procedures would assist both individual teachers and departments in reviewing existing practice.

Teachers need a forum in which their concerns can be heard. Examples of 'good classroom practice' in the key areas could be established in order to encourage their wider adoption. Observations by teachers in each other's classrooms would also make an effective contribution. Subject teachers within their departments could clarify their aims and evaluate their courses in relation to the needs of the pupils. This type of built-in evaluation could be most beneficial in providing for the needs of both experienced and inexperienced teachers.

There is a need to provide INSET relating to mixed-ability teaching, in order to assist teachers to acquire the necessary teaching techniques. This could lead to teachers approaching the teaching of these pupils with greater confidence and understanding. This provision could be offered by the local education authority.

The findings from the study implied strongly that the class teacher must largely assume the responsibility for ensuring that the learning the children are receiving is appropriate to their needs. However, the head of special needs can have an influential role in an organisational and consultative capacity, coordinating with subject departments and the senior management team to effect changes in practice and provision that will assist the pupils' access to ordinary curriculum. Developing a 'whole school' policy and establishing firm guidelines to assist teachers can emphasise the notion that these pupils' learning needs are every teacher's responsibility.

In conducting small-scale research, the most significant aspect of being a teacher/researcher has been its personal value to me. I have had an opportunity to gain insights, broaden perspectives and increase my understanding of classroom life. Choosing to study an area that engages interest is essential. My intention from the beginning was to investigate a group of pupils operating in the comprehensive system to find out how the school meets their educational needs. I feel satisfied that I have fulfilled this objective.

The study has created a link on both a professional and informal basis with the school. The research element has enabled me to increase my understanding of the classroom environment as experienced by both pupils and teachers. Furthermore, it provided me with an opportunity to compare the learning environments and learning experiences of secondary aged pupils in a school for moderate learning difficulties (where I teach) and with those of the pupils attending the local comprehensive. Finally, the process of the study provided occasions to reflect on teacher practice in relation to pupils with special needs and the quality of the learning provided for them.

References

Allen, J. D. (1986), 'Classrom management: students' perspectives, goals and strategies', *American Educational Research Journal*, **23**(3), 437–59.
ACE (1983), *Summary of the 1981 Act* (London: ACE).
Cohen, L. and Manion, L. (1985), *Research Methods in Education* (London: Croom Helm).
DES (1978), *Special Educational Needs* (Warnock Report) (London: HMSO).
Hargreaves, D. H. (1984), *Improving Secondary Schools* (London: ILEA).
Hook, C. (1981), *Studying Classrooms* (Victoria: Deakin University Press).
Johnson, R. and Johnson, D. (1983), 'Effects of co-operative, competitive and individualistic learning experiences on social development', *Exceptional Children*, **49**(4), January. 323–9.
Lincoln, Y. and Guba, E. (1985), *Naturalistic Inquiry* (Beverly Hills, Calif.: Publications).
Madden, N. A. and Slavin, R. W. (1983), 'Mainstreaming students with mild handicap, academic and social outcomes', *Review of Educational Research*, **53**(4), 519–69.
Rosenshine, B. (1983), 'Teaching functions in Instructional Programmes', *Elementary School Journal*, **38**(4), 335–351.

CHAPTER 7

The Most Severe Learning Difficulties: Does Your Curriculum 'Go Back Far Enough'?

Dave Hewett

This paper is potentially about all sorts of things, but in my mind as I started planning it I felt that it was mostly to be an opportunity for me to write about what I think is good, effective practice in my chosen field of work. It was also to be about what we practitioners could or should do in order to continue to develop our work.

I have two main purposes in this regard. The first is likely to be of greatest interest to those who work within the realm of severe learning difficulties, though before other teachers stop reading I tentatively suggest that there may be some generalisable educational truths inherent in discussion of what is otherwise a highly specialised curriculum aimed at a specific pupil group. This intent may roughly be summarised as drawing the attention of teachers of those with the most severe leaning difficulties to the prospect that there may be approaches to working with such pupils that are not based on principles that I crudely and with a little tongue in cheek describe as 'Skinnerism' and 'SAM'ism (see Gardner *et al.*, 1983). Furthermore, curriculum development could and should take place in classrooms as part of the everyday practice of teaching. This is my second intent: I wish to assure other teachers that taking more control over the development of your teaching (including, yes, the theoretical and academic background to it) is not only worthwhile in terms of the potential to serve your pupils better, but is also potentially reassuring and confidence-building for you the teacher. I have also found it great fun.

This form of professional self-assertion has been termed simply and appropriately 'practical action research' (Carr and Kemmis, 1983). Beware, however – such teacher activity can have its own momentum and may become what Carr and Kemmis term 'technical action research', where the aim is to make a more generalised development of educational practice and to encourage others to do the same. I suppose that is what I am doing. In this respect I am merely reiterating the sentiments of many contemporary educationalists from my own experience. The Cambridge Institute plays an overt role in this movement, and was certainly instrumental in encouraging me to develop an interest in this way of thinking.

Background: what to teach – and how?

First of all I would like to orientate readers as to 'where I am coming from'. I am going to do this first of all by recounting just a few anecdotal incidents from experience. If readers cannot produce similar memories I will be surprised.

I came into the work in special schools for pupils with severe learning difficulties (ESNs then) with no basic knowledge whatever – I trained to teach secondary English. It took me years to reach a position where I felt that I had at last compensated for my lack of knowledge about how and what to teach people with mental handicaps (that makes it sound like I feel I now know for certain, which isn't the case). Much earlier than this I had realised that very many teachers I worked with probably did not know too much either, but were blessed with more proficiency than I at giving the appearance that they did. For some years therefore I participated in teaching activities whose purpose I did not fully understand. I feel that this situation is much more likely to pertain when one is working with pupils with the most fundamental and seemingly intractable learning difficulties – the ones that you cannot even dominate enough to get them to sit down and do some threading or an inset puzzle.

I often feel that one of the reasons for the popularity of self-care work with such pupils is that it is so tangible. Who would challenge the purposefulness of something that is so obviously beneficial to an individual? 'Well, he still stays in the corner flapping all day, but he know to hand up his coat and he signs for the toilet on 25 out of 31 occasions.'

Of course I am being overly cynical for effect here, and must apologise to those practitioners who feel maligned by the above statement. I must also stress that I am by no means suggesting that social skills or self-help work based on task analysis should not be carried out. What I am suggesting however, and recent experience assures me that many other teachers and other practitioners share this feeling, is that the highly structured curricula that are available to assist and promote such teaching should be placed properly within an identification of the priorities of learning needs for each individual. Very often, and this is certainly the case with a majority of students in the special school of which I am headteacher, the absolute priority should be the development of communication.

In this context I use the word 'communication' advisedly. What I mean by it is that the word embraces not only the development of the use of speech or symbols, but also the ability to be social as an absolute precursor to communication, and the cognitive attainments that accompany sociability. These attainments are presumably in the realm of growth of understanding of the immediate environment and crucially an understanding of the role and potential of other people within the environment. In our school, when we are working with pupils whose communicative ability is analogous to that of an infant of a few months, we do not make a distinction between cognitive attainments and other attainments. In my mind, therefore, I see a growth in the ability to be social as a cognitive attainment, in that new understanding has developed.

Surely few would disagree with the paramount importance of the facility to communicate, and one would expect the teaching of communication to receive an appropriate stress in actual classroom practice. However, Evans and Ware (1987), in a survey of 'special care' classrooms, found that greater emphasis was placed on other curriculum areas such as physical and social skills. One reason for this may simply be that, though most teachers would agree that this area of the curriculum is of 'prime importance' (Ouvry, 1987), not enough is yet known about how to teach communicative behaviour to pupils who are still in a pre-verbal stage. It is also a curriculum area where it is doubtful that behavioural methods are appropriate (Kiernan, 1984, 1988).

In my estimation, published structured curricula aimed at severe learning difficulties are particularly hazy in this area, though I must mention the recent books by Carol Ouvry (1987) and Judy Sebba (1988), and work by Coupe, Barber and Murphy (1988) who have stressed the importance of positive interaction in the development of communication skills, though a detailed methodology is not elaborated. These writers are starting to look at the work of researchers who study the development of communication in interaction in early infancy. So too is Kiernan (1988), who nominates the motivation to communicate to be of crucial importance, and it seems to me that the drawbacks of a task analysis approach in this regard are obvious.

Kiernan goes on to discuss the possible future potential of teaching methods based on the work of researchers such as Bruner (1975), where the development of communication in the infant is seen as occurring in interpersonal situations by an accumulative process of interaction between the infant and caregivers. This indeed is the area of endeavour that the staff in my school have focused on, following the early work of psychologist Gary Ephraim (1979) in Springfield School, Leavesden Hospital, who postulated and commenced work on a model of teaching based on analysis of how infant learning seems to occur in processes of caregiver–infant interaction. Action research was carried out at Springfield School by Fyfe (1980) and Davis (1985).

The innovation: taking the curriculum farther back

Work in my own school (Harperbury Hospital School, Hertfordshire), on a curriculum founded on theories of early interaction, was primed by a short course given by Gary Ephraim in 1983. The developmental work by staff gathered pace slowly at first. It was not until two years later that we felt that we had achieved some understanding of what we were trying to do and how to do it, and were achieving results with students who had been pathologically 'difficult to reach'. During five years this developmental work has progressed from being an interesting teaching option that we tinkered with through being the subject of absorbing action research, to becoming a force that has radically altered the curriculum of the school, its atmosphere and organisation, and now involves us in formal research. The Cambridge Institute is responsible for assisting this process.

Now, I know that I have yet to explain and illustrate our teaching approach in this chapter. I will do so briefly, in order to make room for my second major intent concerning the benefits of promoting a 'culture of development' in a school. For those specialist practitioners who would like to examine this teaching approach in more detail, I would suggest that you read Nind and Hewett (1988) or Hewett and Nind (1989). A warning here though is that you still may find these papers to be an inadequate description of the teaching. We are aware that one of the contrasting features of this approach by comparison with other, highly structured curricula is that it does not lent itself easily to description in the written word.

Briefly, then, we are concerned with promoting development in young people whose understanding of the immediate environment is very limited – so limited that some are unable to interact with other human beings in any sense meaningfully, whilst others may do so in a restricted, often hopeless, manner. Many of our young people have lifestyles characterised by stereotyped, ritualistic behaviour, and/or extremely challenging anti-social behaviour.

To put it crudely, we have a school with a concentration of pupils of the sort who are found in community schools for severe learning difficulties in smaller numbers. They are the ones who stand in the corner of the classroom flapping hands and leaping up and down, sitting perhaps only for drink and biscuit; the ones who rock, stare remotely into space, rejecting the advances of others; the ones who have a special welfare; the ones teachers have in their class in turns; the ones who cause a school to have a high staff turnover; and the ones who may be able to move only their eyes with any degree of true control from a permanently harnessed or supine position. We have other pupils with a wide range of abilities, but perhaps 60–70 per cent are in this broad grouping.

The approaches we use address what we believe is their central learning need – that they should develop a better understanding of their immediate environment, with the stress on developing better understanding of the other people in the environment, and desiring to be social with them. We try to do it by emulating or borrowing from the way that interpersonal understanding has been identified as arising within the interactive sequences of infancy, according to recent research (a single accessible reference for some of this research is the collection of papers edited by Schaffer, 1977).

We attempt to engage our pupils in one-to-one interactive games where the accent is very much on pleasure first and foremost. For many, simply attracting and keeping the attention of the pupils – making an engagement – is extremely difficult, and early engagements may be short. However, the intention is that engagements based on pleasurable games become longer and more numerous, and that the behaviour within these game situations become more and more sophisticated. As in the 'natural model' of infancy, we find that it is necessary for staff to 'modify' their voice, their facial expressions and their body postures in order to make themselves attractive to the pupils. This is all done with playfulness uppermost, but also extreme sensitivity to the signals and feedback of the pupil – a very fine 'tuning in'. Equipment or toys may be involved, but the basic, most wonderful and flexible piece of equipment that a classroom possesses is the teacher, his or her face, voice and body. We use good interactive computer software too, but the very best software that can be devised does not approach the ability of the teacher to be sensitive and flexible, to behave contingently, and to enter into an interweaving of behaviour with the pupil.

I am sure many teachers will be thinking, 'Well, I play with my lot like that', or 'That's just basic relating; of course you need to do that in order to be with them'. I agree that you can see this happening incidentally in our schools. What I would suggest, however, is that teachers examine carefully the developmental possibilities of that play or that method of relating. Are those occurrences happening spontaneously around the periphery of a basically skills-based, tasks analysis type curriculum? Are these experiences proceeding undocumented and unplanned? Perhaps it is worth documenting and structuring somewhat the intentions in this play, or, further still, consider moving, as we did, these exciting activities from the periphery of the curriculum to the core.

This need not mean doing away with your SAM or EDY curriculum entirely, but it will probably make you re-evaluate it, and it may enhance your teaching of it. Furthermore, to allude again to my earlier reference to Kiernan on motivation, in our school we believe that the motivation for the pupil within such a teaching approach is intrinsic. The motivation is first and foremost enjoyment. We all wish to repeat pleasurable experiences. It may also be, and we cannot yet substantiate this, the thrill of discovery. We believe we are able to perceive our pupils displaying a new and genuine interest in their surroundings, particularly in the people in proximity. We think that our curriculum now 'goes back far enough' in developmental terms. We feel that, formerly, many of the activities we were offering were too advanced for young people who simply did not have the ability to be with another person successfully.

To conclude this section, I would like to do two things. First, I would warmly recommend a paper by Roy McConkey (1989) to back up my view on the potential of play and game, and, to illustrate the recent general interest in the use of human interactions as a teaching force in special education, a book by McGee *et al.* (1987) in the US. Secondly, I return to my remark in the first paragraph. I have described a specialist curriculum for a specific group, but I hope there are general educational considerations here for all teachers to muse on. These I think are to do with the role of pleasure and game in all learning. Do we all really give enough regard to the need intrinsically to motivate our pupils to learn? Or do we mostly decide, in advance, precisely what it is they are going to learn and even precisely how they are going to learn it?

Doing that curriculum development thing

Prior to the developments that are mainly the subject of this chapter, we had a curriculum in our school that was, as with many such curricula, heavily influenced by the principles of behavioural psychology and the tenets of behaviour modification. We attempted to teach life-enhancing skills such as self-help; we attempted, often successfully, to eradicate anti-social behaviours; we did table-based 'cognitive' activities with inset puzzles and other equipment; we attempted to teach awareness of others through various sorts of group work; and we chucked in a bouquet garni of minibus trips, getting in the swimming pool, doing things with paint and so on. (Actually, the bouquet garni is not much different even now. Our most hilarious discussions often concern the 'art' curriculum – we are unsure of our ability to deliver aesthetic activities convincingly.)

I have probably already made it quite clear that I have always been intuitively dissatisfied with teaching approaches for such students that are based solely on behavioural technology; working with such programmes just did not seem to 'fit' with my personality. I did not enjoy the teaching very much, finding the rigidity of the teaching programmes pedantic and irritating. I did not enjoy eradicating behaviours for which I did not have a readily taught substitute. I suppose also, to come clean entirely, I am not amongst the most organised and fastidious of teachers, so such work brought the methodology into direct confrontation with that aspect of my personality. I acknowledge that more methodical practitioners than I may give a more optimistic account of the benefits of such teaching approaches.

My sense of unease is only enhanced when a whole school curriculum is virtually underpinned by these principles. My own experience of meeting other practitioners in similar settings informs me that many others shared this view or feeling. They shared with me too the sensation of being the entuhsiastic practitioner who is academically gauche and, therefore, disabled in any attempt to argue for alternatives, indeed to even consider what alternatives there might be.

This, then, is part of the background to my entry to a one-year diploma course at the Cambridge Institute of Education. Having the opportunity to study in the area of my unease for a whole, blissful year was one of the factors that brought about large-scale change in the curriculum of my school, but it was not the only factor, and not the most important one.

The staff of my school are flexible and questing, and it is this pre-disposition to change that is singularly important. There is no more fundamental change in a school than to alter the course of the curriculum. To some extent, the school already possessed what Holly and Hopkins (1988) term a 'development culture', which allows a school to be 'conducive to growth' (HMI, 1977, quoted in Holly and Hopkins, 1988). My contribution to the radical shift that was to take place in our school curriculum was not so much the developmental work on the curriculum theory and practice, for the development of practice was already occurring within the school. It was more a sort of theoretical, academic corroboration and back-up of the work being developed by rule of thumb in the classrooms. In short, a year of study around my work enabled me to feel less academically gauche and disabled in the face of the often technically intimidating teaching theories in our field. I believe furthermore that my growth in confidence enabled other teachers to feel more confident in their ability to deal with theoretical literature critically, and to place faith in their own work within this framework. This is not meant to imply that we are yet anything other than 'babes in the wood' with respect to our research ability and pro-duction of literature, but we at least have the sensation of being in the wood.

Dadds (1986) terms the sort of research I carried out as a part of my course as 'idiosyncratic', being wholly related to my individual con-cerns and to the concerns of my school. She chronicles the difficulties that individual teachers may face in attempting to 'institutionalise' the results of idiosyncratic research – literally to bring about effective change within their school. For teachers seconded to a course, these difficulties include sceptical colleagues, alienation from the culture of the school by absence on a course, lack of consultation with colleagues over the subject to be studied, and change occurring in the course member as a result of the course to which colleagues are, of course, not subject.

I am bound to admit that none of these concerns was identified and consciously dealt with by myself and colleagues prior to or during my secondment. They were probably all adequately addressed by a combination of sheer good fortune and the already open and responsive culture developing within the school. The 'idiosyncratic' work that I carried out as part of my course was a reflection of concerns that we had openly shared within the school for two or more years; as head of the school I had probably more cause to flit in and out than most teachers on secondment; I carried out an action research project within the school with the willing and tolerant assistance of colleagues; and, crucially, the practical work in the classroom was, if anything, developing faster than my studies.

Whilst the approach to the change that was to come about in our school was shambolic in its lack of clear, longitudinal planning, in some respects the innovations were successful because of that. The innovation ultimately was not owned by any single person – there were various stakeholders within the school. Thus there was no sense of the 'hero innovator', and even though I may be seen as a prime mover, there never really was a stage at which I felt that I had to 'sell' the package to the recipients, willing or unwilling. Gross *et al.* (1971) stress that their work showed that educational innovations often failed during the period of supposed implementation. Innovation generally entails complex and often painful and daunting changes in behaviour and it is at this stage, Gross *et al.* found, that many of the teachers fell foul of frustration and other difficulties despite initial enthusiasm. Thus, in our case, I believe that true joint ownership of the innovation has been crucial. When difficulties and frustrations have been encountered, they too belong to all participants, not solely to the person who is promulgating. The motivation for each teacher has been intrinsic. Joint ownership has, I think, also compensated for the absence of coherent planning of the innovation, at least in the early stages. If, at any stage, we were not quite sure where to go next, at least we were not quite sure together.

So I must emphasise that the most crucial factor in my mind that facilitated the development and adoption of the innovation was not the attractive nature of the innovation, nor that we were able to 'justify' it, intellectually and academically, though both of these factors were highly significant; nor was it because we had seen the innovation operating elsewhere. First and foremost it was because the important people who accept and use the innovation were in a frame of mind to do so, whatever the difficulties. This 'culture of development' arose in our school to a greater extent because we had a fortuitous blend of personalities amongst the staff, teachers who were not abashed at being openly self-reflective about their teaching, and who were prepared to put the work into studying it. An ethos of team teaching has also been an encouragement in this regard. Self-reflection is not enough, however; it must be honest. The first step toward reflexivity is owning up when you know that your teaching is not as effective as it could be. This should assist with the motivation required to do something about it.

So what is the moral here? Clearly I cannot pass on our workable formula for bringing about organisational change, because we do not possess one. I suppose it is the sentiment in the previous paragraph: however good your intended innovation is, it will probably not 'stick' unless the users are well motivated to apply it. Therefore, my advice is to spend some time paying attention to the culture in your school and deciding whether it is one that is amenable to change. If it isn't, then it may be worth while paying further attention to the development of strategies that allow for a process of change, even if your intention is simply to do some curriculum development in your own classroom. A little reading can assist immensely, and you can certainly find these arguments, and even some formulas, set out more eloquently and helpfully than I can put them (Reid, Hopkins and Holly, 1987, for instance, is interesting, and readable enough to be at the bedside).

To conclude

I hope I have made it clear that, though I have challenged reliance on the use of highly structured curricula in schools for severe learning difficulties, I am not arguing for *laissez-faire*. Nor am I particularly arguing for less structure in such teaching, though in the ultimate analysis that may be an effect of my argument. The teaching approach that I have described as coming about in our school has a different kind of structure from the detailed pre-structuring of task analysis teaching. It is perhaps more concerned with 'art' than 'mechanics' and stems from the ability of the teacher to utilise some considerable understanding of what is to be undertaken; to combine this understanding judiciously with abilities that are presumably innate in most adults; and to deploy these 'skills' (sic) within an ebb and flow of mutual shared behaviour with the learner. In effect, the practitioner's knowledge provides a set of mental 'templates' concerning how to teach. These 'templates' provide a basis for the teacher's behaviour in multifarious situations within which the ability to improvise around this 'structure' is also important. That is a description of our theory, but it must be said also here that this curriculum needs to be studied further. In particular, its usefulness needs to be investigated by research – our 'rule of thumb' knowledge is ultimately not sufficient. I hope I have conveyed also that this teaching came about because the teachers wished for it and looked for it. It was not an easy process, but the work involved in the development empowered the teachers with the knowledge and confidence necessary to carrying out this new mode of teaching. I believe that the teachers would not have felt so empowered if they had not each been part of a culture of development. Moreover, I hope that this one example may be some inspiration to the reader who would like to do something similar but does not know where to start. Especially I hope that teachers who read this but who do not agree that what I have described sounds like the best practice with those with very severe learning difficulties will none the less feel encouraged to assume more control of developments in their classrooms.

Acknowledgements

I would like to thank staff at Harperbury school, especially Melanie Nind, for their suggestions and help with this paper.

References

Bruner, J. S. (1975), 'The ontogenesis of speech acts', *Journal of Child Language*, 2(1), 1–19.

Carr, W. and Kemmis, S. (1983), *Becoming Critical: Knowing Through Action Research* (Victoria: Deakin University Press).

Coupe, J., Barber, M. and Murphy, D. (1988), *Communication Before Speech* (Beckenham: Croom Helm).

Dadds, M. (1986). 'The school, the teacher researcher and the in-service tutor', in P. Holly and D. Whitehead (eds), *Collaborative Action Research*, Classroom Action Research Network Bulletin No. 7 (Cambridge: Cambridge Institute of Education).

Davis, M. (1985), 'The usefulness of an interactive approach to the education of severely and profoundly handicapped individuals', unpublished dissertation (Hertfordshire College of Higher Education, Wall Hall).

Ephraim, G. W .E. (1979), 'Developmental processes in mental handicap: a generative structure approach', unpublished PhD thesis (Brunel University Department of Psychology).

Evans, P. and Ware, J. (1987), *'Special Care' Provision: The Education of Children with Profound and Multiple Learning Difficulties* (Windsor: NFER–Nelson).

Fyfe, R. (1980), 'An examination of pre-linguistic interactions between adult and child as a means of facilitating communication development in the S.S.N. institutionalised child, unpublished dissertation (Wall Hall College).

Gardner, J., Murphy, J. and Crawford, J. (1983), *The Skills Analysis Model: An Effective Curriculum for Children with Severe Learning Difficulties* (Kidderminster: BIMH).

Gross, N., Giacquinta, J. B. and Bernstein, M. (1971), *Implementing Organisational Innovations* (London: Harper & Row with the Open University).

Hewett, D. and Nind, M. (1989), 'Developing an interactive curriculum for pupils with severe and complex learning difficulties: a classroom process', in B. Smith (ed.), *Interactive Approaches to the Education of Children with Severe Learning Difficulties* (Birmingham: Westhill College).

HMI (1977), *Ten Good Schools* (London: HMSO).

Holly, P. and Hopkins, D. (1988), 'Evaluation and school improvement', *Cambridge Journal of Education*, 18 (2), 221-45.

Kiernan, C. (1984), 'The behavioural approach to language development', in D. Fontana (ed.), *Behaviourism and Learning Theory in Education* (Edinburgh: Scottish Academic Press).

Kiernan, C. (1988), 'Assessment for teaching communication skills', in J. Coupe and J. Goldbart, *Communication Before Speech* (Beckenham: Croom Helm).

McConkey, R. (1989), 'Interaction: the name of the game', in B. Smith (ed.), *Interactive Approaches to the Education of Children with Severe Learning Difficulties* (Birmingham: Westhill College).

McGee, J. J., Menolascino, F. J., Hobbs, D. C. and Menousek, P. E., (1987), *Gentle Teaching: A Non-Aversive Approach to Helping Persons with Mental Retardation* (New York: Human Sciences Press).

Nind, M. and Hewett, D. (1988), 'Interaction as curriculum', *British Journal of Special Education*, 15 (2), 55-7.

Ouvry, C. (1987). *Educating Children with Profound Handicaps* (Kidderminster: BIMH).

Reid, K., Hopkins, D. and Holly, P. (1987), *Towards the Effective School* (Oxford: Blackwell).

Schaffer, H. R. (ed.) (1977), *Studies in Mother–Infant Interaction* (London: Academic Press).

Sebba, J. (1988), *The Education of People with Profound and Multiple Handicaps* (Manchester: Manchester University Press).

CHAPTER 8

Centres for Integration – A Role for the Special School?

Steve Cochrane

Background

Sixteen years ago, in the concluding chapter of her report of a large-scale research project into the integration of disabled pupils into mainstream schools, Anderson (1973) posed the question:

> 'If increasing numbers of disabled children are placed in ordinary schools, what will be the role of the special schools?'

Sixteen years later, the question is apparently still as relevant, and still, seemingly, as far from being conclusively answered. This is certainly the case in regard to my own current place of employment, a special school in a London Borough.

Similarly, at national level, as Swann (1985) indicates, the trend for physically disabled pupils to be educated in mainstream schools has led to the inclusion of increasing numbers of these pupils within the mainstream. A later study by Swann (in Booth and Swann, 1987) began to outline some of the (largely negative) effects of these developments upon the special school.

At the same time, the recent promotion of, and growing interest in, the ideas of conductive education for 'motor disordered' children has, according to Sutton (1986), presented a challenge to what he sees as the new orthodoxy of 'integration' for pupils with physical difficulties. Since the 'purist' philosophy of conductive education (see Cottam and Sutton, 1986), as practised at the Peto Institute in Hungary, requires the segregation of a discrete group of pupils with similar problems, then an apparent conflict with the 'integrationist' position seems to arise. Need this necessarily be so? Indeed, it seems to me that conductive education has made a number of moves that open up further opportunities to include this group of pupils within the mainstream of education, namely to:

- redefine all the problems experienced by the motor disordered child as learning problems, thus placing these problems firmly within the educational context.
- remove the professional barriers between the different disciplines involved in provision for disabled children in the UK (which can cause such fragmentation in the learning experience of those children).
- develop a specific method of education (rhythmical intention) to enable these children to learn movement and the skills of everyday living as part of an integrated cross-curricular approach.
- establish the absolute importance of involving parents, in a very active way and at a very early stage, in assisting the development of their own child.
- provide 'schools' where parents can develop the necessary skills/understanding to make the most of this involvement.

Nevertheless, the impact of these developments on the education of pupils with physical disabilities (which seem to be pulling in opposite directions) has been to set up a tension within this branch of special education which as yet remain unresolved. Meanwhile, within my own school and LEA, an extensive and intensive review of the provision we were making for pupils with physical disabilities identified significant gaps in the continuum of provision we were making to meet the needs of these pupils at a local level, and suggested some ways forward, which included a continued management role for the special school.

My decision to use the school-based inquiry part of my course to further explore the ethical and methodological issues surrounding research in education (through the context of local and national developments in provision for pupils with physical disabilities) arose from the strong elements of classroom research and constant evaluation that permeated the whole course that I attended at the Cambridge Institute of Education. Having been captured early on in the course by the idea of the teacher as researcher, and having, by the end of my inquiry, now been on both the receiving and the 'delivery' end of educational research, I feel I have reached my own conclusion to the question of whether it is possible to have 'neutral', 'objective' research. Is the researcher unavoidably precipitated into interaction with the subjects of that research, or is it possible to maintain a detached, controlled (controlling?) relationship . . . and if so, what are the ethical/political implications attendant upon his/her involvement? Also, what are the moral/ethical implications of segregating a group of disabled pupils as the subjects of a sustained period of action research – such as that carried out at the Peto Institute in Hungary and in various British institutions under the banner of conductive education?

Research design

My own research stance could broadly be defined as a 'soft-nosed logical positivist' approach, as identified by Miles and Huberman (1984). This approach starts from the assumption that some of the phenomena investigated in the field by social scientists have an objective reality, while others are 'social realities' – existing only because we agree that they exist. What this means in research terms is that Miles and Huberman set out to make their findings from the qualitative data analysis process replicable by other researchers, much as quantitative researchers attempt to do.

Throughout my inquiry, I leaned heavily upon the methodological framework that Miles and Huberman developed to be consistent with this approach. Central to this framework is the 'constant comparative method of qualitative data analysis' – constantly comparing new data, as it is gathered, with the developing theory implicit in a developing set of data-coding categories – first developed by Glaser and Strauss (1967). However, in the main, the methods of actual data gathering will be fairly familiar to anyone who has engaged in any qualitative research.

I took as my ethical starting point the principles laid down by Kemmis and McTaggart (1981) and Elliott (1981), which essentially codify the commitment to negotiation and collaboration with the people who would, in the positivist tradition, have been the subjects of my research. This ethical/political position was further extended during the course of my inquiry to recognition of, and commitment to, the principle of what Lather (1986) calls 'empowerment' – i.e. that the intention and (hopefully) the effect of research upon the subjects of that research should be to increase their understanding of, and ability to affect, their own social situation.

The sites used to make up the data base for my theory development were:

School A, a secondary-age community school in one of the 'Shires', with disabled pupils on roll;
School B, a primary school with disabled pupils on roll, which is within the same Shire LEA;
School C, an all-age day special school for pupils with physical difficulties in a neighbouring Shire, which operates an integration scheme at upper school level;
School D, an all-age boarding school for pupils with physical difficulties in a third Shire, which operates an integration scheme at secondary level;
School E, an all-age day special school in a London borough, which is involved in the integration of disabled pupils at all ages.

Only schools B and C were used formally for any extensive research during this inquiry, though formal information gathering was carried out at school A for a short time. I feel justified in including schools D and E in my data base since I found that during my analysis I was using my experience/observations in these other schools for comparison purposes, and therefore thought it best to make this 'hidden' part of my data base more explicit. Consequently, there are many data gaps for some of these schools, since I was not pursuing systematic research there. Where this is the case, I have indicated this in my text.

Lastly, my research method was what Peter Holly, a tutor at the Cambridge Institute of Education, refers to as 'grounded in literature' – i.e. the literature search took place neither before nor after the empirical research phase, but was an integral part of that phase, informing it and shaping/being shaped by it.

'Negotiation, reciprocity, empowerment'

Robson *et al.* (1987), adapting the work of Fullan (1982), describe change in education as a process involving 'ambiguity, ambivalence and uncertainty' for the individual about the meaning of that change, and suggest that effective implementation is, in effect, a process of clarification.

Special education, along with the mainstream, is going through a period of rapid, and perhaps fundamental, change. The accuracy of the assertion made by Robson and colleagues became rapidly apparent as my excursions into the field brought me into contact with a wide range of individuals, in different institutions, all of whom were dealing with, or attempting to deal with, 'ambiguity, ambivalence and uncertainty' in their working lives. They were all engaged in the process of clarification – finding personal meaning in the changes they were experiencing – whether in isolation, or through interaction with their colleagues . . . a process to which I, too, was a party.

My own part in what came increasingly to be a collaborative process is perhaps best described by Lather (1986), in a paper that itself came to me during a site visit, in the course of my interaction with a teacher at that school. Lather's attempt to discover personal meaning (i.e. an 'emancipatory' approach to research in what she describes as an unjust world) struck a chord with my own experience.

She suggests that we should attempt to develop research that is aimed at encouraging self-reflection and deeper understanding on the part of the persons being researched as well as on the part of the researcher. Such an inquiry should, to maintain internal consistency and ethical integrity, be characterised by 'negotiation, reciprocity, empowerment'. In other words, researcher and informants should engage in a process of give and take and negotiation, which should result in an increase in knowledge, understanding and the capacity to take effective action, for both parties.

If these then are my research aims, clarified over the period of this inquiry, then fairly obviously my research makes no attempt to be 'neutral'. I have a commitment to changing the status quo in education, particularly in respect of those who are disadvantaged within our educational system for one reason or another. In this I have been encouraged during my research by the extent to which this commitment is shared by so many of the people who work in the field of education.

However, my commitment to change does not mean that I am committed to change for change's sake. For, if we are concerned with quality in education, then, as Fullan (1982) says, how do we know when change is worthwhile, and on which occasions rejection, rather than adoption, of a proposed educational initiative ensures greater quality of education? This is particularly relevant in the UK at the present time, with a host of new educational initiatives over the past few years still largely unassimilated into many institutions, and with these initiatives now being closely followed by the new National Curriculum.

In education, we need to be able to evaluate proposed initiatives/programmes before they have gone too far along the road of implementation, and before possibly irreparable damage has been done to children's life chances. This is not to minimise the need for long-term evaluation to be carried out as well, but it does mean that we cannot, as responsible educationists, make professional commitment to any proposals unless those changes have meaning for us, i.e. unless we are professionally convinced that they are worth trying. For my own 'rule of thumb', I have decided to look for evidence not only of good intentions, but also of the capacity on the part of the planners to think through the implementation phases so that, as Fullan (1982) argues should happen, the changes have meaning to all involved in them.

So, what meanings did I find, during the course of my inquiry, that I was then able to share (and validate?) with my site informants, colleagues and tutors? Returning to my original purpose in beginning this inquiry, what did I find out that may be of use in planning for the development of our own LEA provision.

The overview

My research identified three analytical elements – management, support mechanisms, learning environments – which provide the overall framework within which to develop my theory (see Figure 8.1). I will now consider each of them in turn.

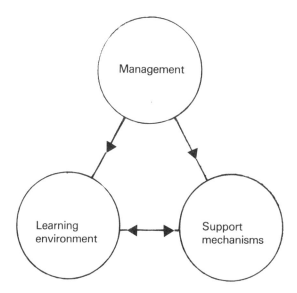

Figure 8.1 Significant factors in the integration of disabled pupils

Management

In looking at management as a factor in the planning of our own institutional development, I have adopted the 'Seven S' model of Athos and Pascale (1981), but have made one amendment, which will I think assist with clarity without sacrificing memory aid provided by alliteration. This change is simply to substitute the term 'shared vision' for 'superordinate values', since this term is one that came out of my field work, and perhaps better describes the nature of the phenomenon within an educational setting. I therefore offer my amended model as a framework within which to analyse and plan the management of an integration scheme (see Figure 8.2).

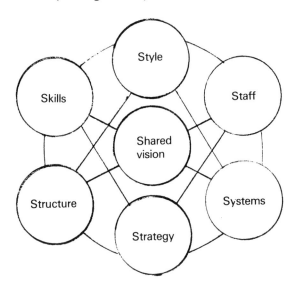

Figure 8.2   Revised 7S managerial molecule
Source: Adapted from Athos and Pascale (1981)

The importance of good management to the maintenance of a good working atmosphere for both pupils and staff (as identified by Rutter *et al.*, 1979) was highlighted by the superintendent physiotherapist from my own school after her visit to school B, when she commented 'I was impressed by the happy atmosphere throughout the school. It seemed to me that the children were getting a pretty good deal . . . the resource team leader was key. She seemed to have eyes everywhere . . . ' – a view that was confirmed by my own observations and the comments of every single member of staff I interviewed.

However, management is not solely about personalities, nor is it solely about the effectiveness of departmental managers. For children to 'get a good deal' seems to require a consistency and competence, not to mention imagination, at school and LEA management levels as well. For instance, the best examples I saw of management practice showed evidence of imaginative and competent performance from LEA officers, and from the headteacher of the school, as well as exceptional ability and dedication at departmental level too. Perhaps, needless to say, this trend towards excellence (and the commitment to making integration work) did not stop with the management team, but was carried forward by all of the staff working with them, whether from inside or outside the school. It provided ample evidence of the crucial concept of *shared vision* and of well-developed *strategies* to go with it.

The essentially multidisciplinary nature of the planning of provision for this group of pupils means that there is no clear, direct *line management structure* and that some sort of *network management structure* has perforce to exist. The participative, democratic management *style* needed to operate successfully within this sort of organisational framework was present in the most successful examples of good practice – though not always evident at LEA office level, where the management style still tended to be fairly autocratic. This, to Fullan (1982), was one of the key issues in the management of change – the tension between what he calls 'fidelity' (or attempting to achieve homogeneous change in a number of situations) and adaptation or variation to suit local circumstances – and is perhaps reflected in the tension between line and network management demands and between autocratic and democratic management styles.

Whatever the reasons, the management task facing school C was, despite the smaller number of children and probably the same number of staff, considerably more complex than that facing the management of school B. This was despite the fact that the headteacher of school B agreed that his own role and power–dependency relationships were now much closer to the model proposed by Bowers (1984a) for special schools (see Figure 8.3, which describes a high level of dependency upon external agencies for the headteacher) rather than the one suggested in the same article as representing primary schools (which typically present the headteacher as mainly dependent upon his/her teaching staff).

A large part of the complexity for school C, which being a special school exhibited the full range of dependency relationships indicated

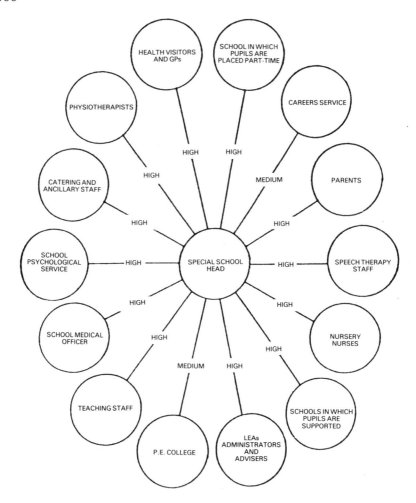

Figure 8.3 Power-dependency model for special schools
Source: Bowers (1984a)

in Figure 8.3, came from the increased requirements for network management techniques in the relationship with the mainstream schools that acted as part-time hosts for school C's pupils. The problems of developing and maintaining an effective communication *system* within a mainstream setting seemed less daunting where they were not further compounded by relations with a separate special school.

The question of each of the schools possessing, maintaining and developing appropriate specialised *skills* proved to be a particularly sensitive one in most schools. It did seem to be recognised and fairly successfully answered, in terms of *staffing* policy towards both recruitment and staff development, in the best examples that I saw.

In general, the problems being faced by schools C, D and E seemed to correspond very closely to those identified by Dessent (in Bowers, 1984b) in his analysis of special schools attempting to operate as resource centres for mainstream schools. In the end, I found myself coming to agree more wholeheartedly with his assertion that the phenomenon of special schools acting in this way was a temporary one. The success I have seen in schools A and B and in the host schools for school E has led me to believe that this phase is passing.

If mainstream schools are resourced and supported properly by LEA and school management, and also, as crucially, by central government, then I see no reason why they should not be capable of taking account of a much wider range of individual differences than is currently thought possible. The key questions seem to be of *timing* – how rapidly can this transfer of resources, expertise and, most importantly, responsibility be realistically and sensitively carried out with 'negotiation, reciprocity and empowerment' – and of the *commitment* on the part of the LEA, and of central government, to carry it through within the context of the new National Curriculum.

The learning environment

The term 'learning environment', as used here, applies to the social, academic and physical aspects of the child's experience. Howarth (1987) stresses the importance of appropriate learning environments for children with special needs (in this case physical disabilities), which she suggests are characterised by:

- a clear understanding of child development;
- flexible learning opportunities for different levels of development within the same class;
- a focus on the classroom as a social group;
- an interdisciplinary approach;
- the opportunity for the child to experience a variety of social groupings and kinds of environment;
- emphasis on the pupil's own activity, and learning by direct experience;
- a thematic rather than subject-based approach;
- clear objectives and priorities for each child.

To this list, Hodgson (1984) would add:

- careful consideration for the physical environment;
- effective assistance with self-care;
- adequate transport.

If we examine the total learning environment in each of the schools, then some very interesting, and perhaps surprising, things emerge.

Taking the physical context first, as perhaps the easiest to deal with, one pattern that emerged was of the difference between the physical accessibility of schools A and B, which were fully adapted and equipped for disabled use, and the incomplete nature of the adaptations and facilities at schools C and D. One common feature in both school A and school B had been a 'fierce' and hard-fought campaign by school governors and management to ensure adequate resourcing for the integration proposals. This did not seem to have happened at school C or at school D, and, indeed, the battle over resources/facilities at school E is still going on – 14 years after the integration scheme began! Whatever the reason, it remains an important factor, since the kind of facilities and access available not only sends messages to disabled pupils concerning their personal value, but can also actively promote or undermine their personal independence or autonomy.

One very interesting discovery was the extent to which (at school B at least) the positive effects of integration had been underestimated by the planners when designing what was obviously originally intended to be a disabled suite or unit within the school. All the disabled facilities had been located together within the school, but were in effect now significantly underused because the disabled pupils preferred to use the adapted toilets in each of the school's regular toilet blocks rather than those in the 'disabled suite'. Also, with an apparent growing trend towards physiotherapy being carried out in the classroom, the physiotherapy room was used less than was at first imagined. This is not to say that a more severely disabled population in later years might not have more need of the specialist resources, but do they all need to be clustered together?

It is impossible really (for any children, but perhaps particularly for disabled children) to separate the social from the academic dimension of the learning environment, since, as Cotton (1984) says, child development is global not linear. Consequently, any division between education, therapy and care is, from the point of view of the child's experience, an artificial one and emotionally damaging. In a similar vein, but coming from another angle, Howarth (1987) argues that: 'The essential basis for human development centres upon the principles and techniques of social interaction, and a satisfactory curriculum is a matter of extending understanding of, and skill in implementing, learning environments of many kinds.' The intertwined nature of social and academic development is further emphasised by Cope and Anderson (1977) and Anderson (1973), who discovered that the acceptability of disabled pupils seems to correlate strongly with them being academically able.

It is a similar understanding of the developmental needs of young children with cerebral palsy that underpins conductive education (see Cottam and Sutton, 1986). This, together with its focus upon *functional* learning rather than abstract treatment, and its recognition that objectives in this direction can best be achieved by limiting the number of specialists involved with the child, are what makes the approach so attractive to me.

Where I part company with conductive education is over its insistence upon a discrete group of pupils with similar problems. The argument over this sort of grouping for other aspects of the curriculum (e.g. reading and writing?) are well rehearsed and, I would have thought, pretty well won in favour of a differentiated curriculum. Although I can see the inspirational advantages of having a group all working towards the same goals, I have seen the same effect being produced in one of school E's host schools, by a class of able-bodied children, with their disabled classmate learning to walk from the class to the hall for assembly by himself. The pure form of conductive education misses out on the benefits of the opportunity to experience different social groupings and learning environments – in other words, the learning that occurs *with* an able-bodied peer group under carefully managed conditions. This, to me, is where its challenge to integration fails. Nevertheless, it still has many important points to make about how we educate this group of children – and indeed about a wider group of the school population (for instance, the 'clumsy' child). Sutton (1986) resolves the matter to his own satisfaction by suggesting that motor disordered children should spend their earliest years in separate provision going through a period of conductive education aimed at facilitating their integration into the mainstream at a later stage and at a higher point on the continuum.

A similar conclusion is reached by Stobart (1986), in another challenge to the new orthodoxy of integration, when writing about the integration of children with some intellectual impairment (which would include many children on the rolls of schools C, D and E). He argues that social integration for these pupils does not occur spontaneously but needs to be structured carefully into classroom organisation (for instance through cooperative learning tasks) and that specific social skills may need to be taught in a separate context before integration is attempted.

Surely, though, it should be possible to 'integrate' the principles behind these 'challenges' into mainstream situations? Much progress has already been made towards the integration of a number of disparate objectives into meaningful learning tasks. For example:

(a) the nationally validated Pre-Vocational Certificate course developed at school A, which is designed to involve both able-bodied and disabled in a programme to promote mutual awareness and capability in functional independence skills.

(b) the classroom in which I spent a couple of hours at school B, where a visually impaired child and a physically disabled child were encouraged to 'develop globally' (an expression from Cotton, 1984) through their active involvement in a range of stimulating and challenging activities, in which they participated upon equal terms with their classmates, but which nevertheless took account of their individual differences.

Howarth (1987) also has a number of practical suggestions of ways that this might be done, as do Thompson *et al.* (1986), Nevin and Thousand (1986), Reister and Bessette (1986), Fagen *et al.* (1986), and Graves *et al.* (1986), which draw from the US experience of 'mainstreaming'. The recent initiatives in pre-vocational education also open up a whole range of possibilities, as discussed in Bailey and Hearn (1988), while the recent concern with personal and social education opens up a further range of possibilities.

These challenges must be healthy if they prevent any descent into complacency and continue to raise expectations of what is possible with disabled children, but, to me, the place to develop special education is in the context of the mainstream, and it is here that resources, as Dessent (in Bowers, 1984b) argues so forcefully, need to be allocated.

Support mechanisms

Support mechanisms, in the context of disabled integration, really need to be examined from the point of view of support for parents of disabled pupils and for teachers of disabled pupils, as well as for the pupils themselves. Information concerning support for and involvement of parents can be found in Howarth (1987) and in Sigston (in Bowers 1987); and suggestions concerning support for teachers abound in Hodgson (1984), Jordan and McLaughlin (1986), Fimian (1986), and Bowers (1987).

Support mechanisms for physically disabled pupils are, by their very nature, multidisciplinary. Bowers (1987) has pointed to the different knowledge bases used by individuals from different disciplines, and Francis *et al.* (1986) noted the differences in language that went with the different conceptual frameworks used by each discipline. Thus communication between members of the national 'multidisciplinary team' emerges as a significant problem right at the outset.

The problems inherent in this are further compounded by the distinction, identified by Bowers (1987), between internal and external support agencies. The problems of individuals with separate line management chains operating within what is (or should be) a network management situation were graphically outlined to me by the headteacher of school B, in the same way as some years previously they had been outlined to me by the deputy headteacher of one of the 'host' schools for pupils from school E. If the line managers of external agents are not aware of, or not sympathetic to, the work of the school, then different (competing?) priorities may be established and conflicting demands may be made upon individuals. Bowers recommends that senior line managers need to resolve these issues directly. In the long term, perhaps we could aim to integrate support mechanisms more fully into the learning environment.

The best examples of good practice came where the support mechanisms were fairly straightforward in their operation, in that the pupils were very clearly the responsibility of the school, and external support agencies were coordinated through the internal support team. Arrangements where pupils remained the responsibility of a special school seemed less effective at offering appropriate support within the mainstream.

One interesting development was occurring in some schools, where, perhaps on the basis that people in the mainstream need to learn about disability as much as (if not more than) disabled people need to learn about their able-bodied peers, they were making efforts to demystify the medical – paramedical process. This they did by having doctors to talk to staff, and by bringing physiotherapy out of the physio room as much as possible and into the classroom. This last move had, according to one headteacher, much to do with class teachers not wanting pupils out of their classes and missing activities for any longer was absolutely necessary.

Trying to find ways round these difficulties is always problematical.

On a practical level, scheduling formal multidisciplinary meetings is always difficult, and this places extra importance upon the informal communication network.

Cotton (1984) has identified the 'linear' approach of each member of a multidisciplinary team as being another obstacle, and offers a possible solution. Traditionally, no recognition is made of the 'global nature' of a child's development, and each specialist works in a linear fashion upon their own chosen aspect of the child's development. Consequently, little attention is usually given to the effect that development in one area may have upon other areas of development. This approach may also mean that a single child with complex needs may be faced with a number of professionals (e.g. teacher, support teacher, welfare assistant, physiotherapist, speech therapist, occupational therapist, doctor/nurse, teacher of the deaf, teacher of the visually impaired, educational psychologist . . . or any combination of the above). This not only tends to undermine the child's sense of security, which is so important to his/her learning and which is fostered through a single or few close relationships, but also greatly exacerbates the communication problems. Cotton's (1984) solution was to propose the development of what she called interdisciplinary teams (IDT's) as a step towards the establishment of transdisciplinary teams (TDT's), and as a replacement for multidisciplinary teams (MDT's), which she saw as being concerned in their formal meetings with retrospective analysis and assessment of the child's development up to that point.

For Cotton, the IDT would differ from the MDT in that it would be goal-oriented (i.e. forward-looking) and would organise each member of the team's contribution towards those goals, while still allowing each member of the team to pursue their own specialism with the child. The developmental stage beyond the IDT, and TDT, would also be goal-oriented, but would differ by the way in which the goals were pursued with the child. Thus, for the TDT, the task would be to select one member of the team who would take responsibility for that child's global development, and that member would then be advised/trained/supported by the other members of the team in carrying out his/her assumed responsibility.

The barriers to this TDT coming into being are identified by Cotton in the same article. These relate quite closely to the problems anticipated by Bowers (1987) as arising from what he calls the difference between 'expressed' and 'core' values, which lead professionals of all disciplines to resent the 'blurring of professional boundaries' even though this may be beneficial to the recipients of the service. Even so, it should be possible to move towards the IDT, but how feasible is it to envisage the development of a TDT within a mainstream setting? If this were to prove possible, it would go a long way towards accommodating the challenge presented by conductive education to integration.

Conclusion

Plainly, the relationship between special school involvement in integration and the maintenance of a high-quality learning environment for disabled pupils is not a direct positive correlation. Indeed, the main difference in the quality of education in integrating schools seems to relate, as elsewhere, to the quality of the management team responsible for those pupils. Certainly there was evidence that, in one school at least, the *absence of the special school*, which might, under my own LEA's planning, have been expected to act as a resource base, *was a positive advantage*. The schools had fully taken on the responsibility for dealing with some of their pupils' very individual needs, and had vastly exceeded the expectations initially held by the pre-existing special school and the LEA that did the planning.

Now, of course, the full continuum of provision (needed to match the continuum of needs to be found within my own special school) was not being provided within any of the mainstream schools, but the range of needs was surprisingly broad (including a child with no speech and very little use of limbs, who was fully functionally integrated into a mainstream class, and a girl of 14 years old who was just preparing for secondary transfer). Perhaps the idea of a continuum of provision should not be used as a yardstick when discussing very individual needs that are always contextually defined?

Whatever the case, it was very obvious that first-rate integration practice can occur without any need for special school or service involvement – if the school as a whole is taking on its responsibility for every child. The key here, as the management team in school B were well aware, lies in the development and promotion of 'a whole school approach' to a whole range of issues – so that, whatever whole school policy is planned, the issue of special educational needs is seen by all staff as being of central importance.

My basic feeling then, at the end of this inquiry, is one of optimism concerning the future of education for pupils with disabilities – tinged with a note of caution under the expected impact of the new National Curriculum (still a matter for much speculation at the time of writing). However, what seems to remain as the biggest barrier to full integration for all the pupils currently on our roll is the curriculum that exists in the mainstream at the moment – and by curriculum I mean all the learning experiences, both planned and unplanned, as part of both the formal and hidden curriculum, that are offered to disabled pupils. All the issues of physical access, adequate facilities and effective support can be, and in many cases are being, satisfactorily resolved, but the match between the pupil and the learning task, in a situation where that pupil can also have access to an able-bodied peer group, remains the hardest thing to achieve.

A common curriculum framework for mainstream and special schools – as suggested by Wilson (1981) and given form by many of the new curriculum initiatives (e.g. CPVE, TVEI, GCSE and school A's pilot Pre-Vocational Certificate), which so closely resemble curricular suggestions made by Anderson and Clarke (1982), Hutchinson and Tennyson (1986) and Howarth (1987) to meet the needs of just the client group under discussion in this chapter – could provide a sympathetic climate for the necessary developments to occur. However, within this climate, recognition needs to be made that:

● Special schools have a 'limited shelf life', and will be phased out entirely within a defined time-scale – and that decision needs to be taken at central government level as well as at LEA level.
● During this 'hand-over' period, full responsibility for all aspects of the management of the learning environment and support mechanism for disabled pupils will, in planned phases, be transferred to the mainstream schools selected as the initial 'resource bases'.
● The change needs to be:
 (a) adequately and consistently resourced and supported by the LEA,
 (b) characterised by a policy of 'negotiation, reciprocity and empowerment' towards the staff in both the mainstream (who will be assuming new responsibilities) and in the special school (whose change in working life will be a fundamental one).
 In other words, HOW the change is implemented is as important as the direction in which it will be going.
● Parents and the pupils themselves will need to be informed, listened to and fully involved in the process – which requires a recognition on the part of the planners that, to quote Robson *et al.* (1987), they must not assume that their 'version of what the change should be is the one that should/could be implemented'.

In short, we have to exchange our view of what should be through *interaction* with others concerned.

References

Anderson, E. (1973), *The Disabled Schoolchild* (London: Methuen).

Anderson, E. and Clarke, L. (1982), *Disability in Adolescence* (London: Methuen).

Athos, A. G. and Pascale, R. T. (1981), *The Art of Japanese Management* (London: Allen Lane).

Bailey, T. and Hearn, M. (1988) 'Enfield TVEI goes "special" ', *British Journal of Special Education*, **15**(1).

Booth, T. and Swann, W. (eds.) (1987), *Including Pupils with Disabilities* (Milton Keynes: Open University Press).

Bowers, T. (1984a), 'Power and Conflict: facts of life', in T. Bowers (ed.), *Management and the Special School* (London: Croom Helm).

Bowers, T. (ed.) (1984b), *Management and the Special School* (London: Croom Helm).

Bowers, T. (ed.) (1987), *Special Educational Needs and Resource Management* (London: Croom Helm).

Cope, C, and Anderson, E. M. (1977), *Special Units in Ordinary Schools: an exploratory study of special provision for disabled children* (London: Institute of Education).

Cottam, P. and Sutton, A. (1986), *Conductive Education: A System for Overcoming Motor Disorder* (London: Croom Helm).

Cotton, E. (1984), 'Integration of disciplines in the treatment and education of children with Cerebral Palsy', in S. Levitt (ed.), *Paediatric Development Therapy* (London: Blackwell).

Elliott, J. (1981), 'Action research: a framework for self-evaluation in schools (Cambridge Institute of Education, mimeo).

Fagen, S. *et al.* (1986), 'Reasonable mainstreaming accommodations for the classroom teacher', *The Pointer*, **31**(1). 4–7.

Fimian, M. (1986), 'Social support, stress, and special education teachers: improving the work situation', *The Pointer*, **31**(1).

Francis, E. *et al.* (1986), 'Communication for special educational needs: a multidisciplinary approach', *British Journal of In-Service Education*, autumn. 133–139.

Fullan, M. (1982), *The Meaning of Educational Change* (New York: Teachers' College Press).

Glaser, B. and Strauss, A. (1967), *The Discovery of Grounded Theory* (New York: Aldine).

Graves D. *et al.* (1986), 'Reasonable accommodations for students with organizational problems', *The Pointer*, **31**(1). 8–11.

Hodgson, A. (1984), 'Integrating physically handicapped pupils', *Special Education: Forward Trends*, **11**(1).

Howarth, S. (1987), *Effective Integration: Physically Handicapped Children in Primary Schools* (Windsor: NFER–Nelson).

Hutchinson, D. and Tennyson, C. (1986), *Transition to Adulthood* (London: FEU).

Jordan, T. and McLaughlin (1986), 'Concerns of regular classroom teachers regarding mainstreaming', *The Pointer*, **31**(1).

Kemmis, S. and McTaggart, R. (1981), *The Action Research Planner* (Victoria: Deakin University Press).

Lather, P. (1986), 'Research as praxis', *Harvard Educational Review*, **56** (3).

Miles, M. B. and Huberman, A. M. (1984), *Qualitative Data Analysis* (Beverly Hills: Sage).

Nevin, A. and Thousand, J. (1986), 'What the research says about limiting or avoiding referrals to special education', *Teacher Education and Special Education*, **9** (4).

Reister, A. and Bessette, K. (1986), 'Preparing the peer group for mainstreaming exceptional children', *The Pointer*, **31** (1).

Robson, C. *et al.* (1987), *In-Service Training and Special Educational Needs: Running Short School-Focused Courses* (Manchester: Manchester University Press).

Rutter, M. *et al.* (1979), *Fifteen Thousand Hours* (London: Open Books).

Stobart, G. (1986) 'Is integrating the handicapped psychologically defensible?' *Bulletin of the British Psychological Society*, **39**.

Sutton, A. (1986), 'Conductive Education: a challenge to integration', *Educational and Child Psychology*, **3**, Pt 2.

Swann, W. (1985), 'Is the integration of children with special educational needs happening? An analysis of recent studies of pupils in special schools', *Oxford Review of Education*, **11**, Pt 1.

Thompson, D. *et al.* (1986), 'Spotlighting positive practices for mainstreaming', *The Pointer*, **31** (1) 34–42.

Wilson, M. (1981), *The Curriculum in Special Schools* (London: Schools Council).

CHAPTER 9

Using Classroom Action Research to Support Curriculum Development and Integration

Brian Steedman

This chapter begins with certain premises. It is my view that the effectiveness of special education has been transformed by its adoption of a behavioural objectives bias in its curriculum (Ainscow and Tweedle, 1979). On the other hand, this has narrowed the focus of its work, provoking criticism of its purpose. It has developed aims and methods separate from those of the mainstream, and this has proved detrimental as increasingly efforts have been directed towards relocating special needs provision within the sector. There is a need to redress this situation.

However, curriculum development is a tough nut to crack, frequently growing out of research that is largely divorced from the classroom. This denies the opportunity for innovation to be shaped specifically for its location and prevents students and teachers from having a say in implications. This denial of a voice underlines the disadvantages of 'change from the top', which characterises much development in education. The overriding premise of this paper is, therefore, that change is an interactive process, out of which, potentially, all participants can learn – that this process is at least as equal in value as its product.

The project described below, therefore, seeks to recognise these concerns. It was committed to widening the curricular options of students and increase their participation in determining the contents of their learning. It was concerned to encourage student's interaction, so that cognition and communication would be enhanced. It promoted process rather than product, and method rather than content. Since it aimed to secure feedback from all participants, it used the technique of triangulated evaluation (Elliott and Adelman, 1976). Lastly, and most importantly, the project sought to have something to offer us in bridging the divide between mainstream and special education, and thus in furthering the process of meeting students' individual needs in both sectors.

Context for the project

'Parkside' is a large special school for children seen to have emotional and behavioural difficulties. Its junior department, to which I belong, has four classes, each of eight children. Two classes attend the school full time, whilst the others spend approximately half of their week in mainstream schools where they are supported by their Parkside class teachers; structured individual learning programmes are used for all students. Where the imposition of this carefully organised curriculum reveals behaviour problems, these in turn are dealt with by use of programmes utilising reinforcement of acceptable behaviour, and these are, wherever possible, carried over into mainstream schools. Such developments have been successful in enabling students to make academic progress, thus increasing confidence in their abilities, and to begin to cope with the mainstream. Gradually, their improving behaviour has increased their acceptability there. Frequently this has led on to successful reintegration.

However, these strategies rely heavily upon the teaching in our primary schools of academic tasks in the morning (when students attend Parkside) and 'recreational' tasks in the afternoon, when they are in mainstream. Increasingly the introduction of topic-based work has broken down this dichotomy, which in any case was never absolute. Often schools have noted students well prepared for concentrating on individual tasks, but unable to cope with situations where they were required to interact with other students and with teachers. Students are ill-prepared for an expanded curriculum aimed at increasing awareness beyond the mastery of basic skills. Additionally, they often do not possess the secretarial and study skills appropriate to this approach. They have difficulties in concentrating on a single didactic signal because active listening is not mastered.

These are the shortcomings that emerged from examining one school's approach. To them must be added the criticisms of the

Warnock Report (DES, 1978), and of Tomlinson (1982), which were especially unhappy about the narrowness of academic work in the special school. A watered-down curriculum was seen as preparing students for only a limiting future. Interestingly, these were criticisms made earlier of similar approaches in the mainstream, which went unheeded. Britton (1970), Barnes *et al.* (1969) and Rosen and Rosen (1973) were all concerned with language development and with student interaction, issues that we now saw as lying at the centre of our students' problems as perceived in their mainstream schools.

Our attempts to address these issues floundered on several counts. The heterogeneous nature of our groups, mixing age and attainment, made whole class teaching difficult. Students continued to work on individual programmes, and thus our 'solutions' revolved around 'bought in' published materials, which required written responses. These naturally made interaction unlikely, and were of little use to students whose reading skills were inadequate. Consequently, we began to look for alternative teaching methods able to be used along-side our existing behavioural objectives approach in order to offer some aid to our students in developing skills of use to them in the mainstream. It was during my year's secondment at the Cambridge Institute of Education that I was able to set up the project that is described below.

The project: background

The work of Johnson and Johnson (1983, 1986) formed the basis of the project. Their group investigation method is characterised by the gathering of data by students working in cooperation together, and interpreting these data through group discussion. Information assembled through this interaction is subsequently made into a group product. Students are organised into small (two–six member) groups, academically and ethnically heterogeneous. Teachers follow the groups' progress closely, offer assistance where necessary, but act as facilitators of learning rather than as controllers. Students attempt to present their findings to their peers in ways that are interesting to them; the groups own their efforts. Follow-up studies suggest that the method is successful: students gain academically and socially, have more contact with teachers, gain in self-esteem, and develop mutual concern. Enjoyment is enhanced (Yeomans, 1983). However, young children need to be taught appropriate 'entry' skills, namely reasoning, listening and sharing (Hockaday, 1984). The opportunity that cooperative group work appeared to offer us to work on a wider and more stimulating curriculum seemed worth trying.

The project: description

The project operated with a group of eight students attending Parkside part time. All were boys, ranging in age from 8 to 11; the group was ethnically mixed. Subsequent decisions about the direction of the project were shared between the class teacher, its welfare assistant and myself. Discussion led to students working in two groups of four with a spread of attainment in secretarial skills and perceived cooperative behaviour. All children scored poorly on standardised reading tests, ranging between reading ages of 6y 7m and 7y 11m (Neale).

A hypothesis was arrived at that we would succeed in providing a heterogeneous group of children with emotional and behavioural difficulties with a wider, awareness-based curriculum in a way that would not detract from their present basic skills programme. This would be done by assigning students to groups so that their combined skills would enable them to develop in independence, cooperation, listening and communication skills. Pupils' interaction would be favourable to their cognitive and language development. The project would be intrinsically rewarding to students. It would also have foreseeable advantages in encouraging students' integration into mainstream schools. We would verify the project's effectiveness by seeking the views of the class teacher and welfare assistant, the students and myself. In practice we did this informally on each day of the project, with our conversations recorded by myself as soon as possible afterwards. On completion of the project, taped interviews were also conducted with students.

The project operated two mornings each week for three weeks – a total of about $10\frac{1}{2}$ hours in all. A series of introductory exercises began on the first morning with the aim of introducing the practice of cooperative group working, demonstrating some of the necessary skills, and assessing groups' readiness to participate effectively. These took, first, the form of 'brainstorming', to rehearse the necessity to consider and accept the contribution of all group members. Secondly, the groups worked on 'cloze' procedures, which required them to cooperate on tasks, discuss alternative responses and achieve consensus. These exercises took up only one morning's work. So far as was possible, the three adults involved took no part in the exercises, referring enquiries from groups back upon their own resources.

Equally we allowed groups to exercise their own responsibility for discipline, and for the main part they did this effectively because they were actively engaged and stimulated by their work. We stressed that we would not control wherever possible and that certain normal requirements, such as sitting neatly and quietly on seats and remaining as stationary as possible, were suspended.

Some useful assessment data emerged from this first day. One group worked particularly effectively, with all members taking great care to involve each other and make decisions cooperatively. The second group was more readily dominated by one group member and seemed more concerned with product than process. Decisions were more likely to be taken on the basis of status, and inappropriate responses occurred because of this. Such issues were regularly discussed in feedback sessions, which took place during the class's usual mid-morning break for breakfast.

There was general agreement among the adults that the introductory exercises demonstrated 'good-enough' cooperative skills, and on the second day of the project we moved on to the main task for each group of producing a newspaper. We provided students with some initial information on the nature of newspaper production, with particular emphasis on its cooperative nature. Groups then began their own planning for production, choosing a title and a layout, allocating tasks among members, and roughing out potential stories. By the close of the second morning writing had begun in earnest.

It must be noted that much of this work was barely at a literate level, and progress was only possible with considerable support. To some extent it was possible for students to provide such support for one another, but there was often much inhibition about their competence to produce a 'finished product', which militated against the effectiveness of this. Noteworthy also was the problem that we as adults had in standing back whilst our students struggled with the process of creation, and there were occasions when we offered our services as scribes too readily. That this was the case emerged quite forcefully in our final feedback session, as we shall note below.

Over a period of four further mornings, a rich variety of copy emerged, national and local. 'Ferry disaster' held the front page of *The Sun*, bringing news of the Zeebrugge tragedy, together with 'Microwave madness', a story about cruelty to animals. On the back page, 'Teacher in a spot' told humorously of the eruption of a large boil on the class teacher's nose. Meanwhile, over at *The Advertiser*, the whole front page was given over to a scandal of educational under-

116

resourcing, with the class welfare assistant demanding a new toaster with rumblings of potential strike action. The back page of *The Advertiser* was troublesome until one student, generally a follower rather than a leader, had the brainwave of developing a sports page, and his interest in football rapidly filled the blank space. Adults showed the children how to present the copy newspaper-style, in columns; spaces were juggled and copy expanded or reduced to fit the available inches. Finally, with great industry the papers were 'put to bed.' I took them off to be photocopied in A3 size, and the main exercise of the project was ended.

During the entire project only one serious problem of behaviour occurred, though there were also minor personality clashes, which were no more than to be expected among any normal group of people engaged upon a high-pressure activity – journalism, for example. The serious problem happened on the final morning of production, when one child had to be restrained from attacking another in the playground at the end of a football game. The child, motivated by a need to return to the project, quickly controlled his behaviour.

Finally, a time was set for me to show the students their finished work, and to discuss with them their thoughts on the activity. This I did by allowing their conversations with me to flow as freely as possible. When they had had their say, I covered my outstanding concerns. The children gave their permission for the conversation to be tape recorded.

Feedback

Students unreservedly confirmed that they enjoyed the project. They contrasted it with structured basic skills practice, which they characterised as 'work' and as concerned with product:

'We do it, we get the answers.'

Further, in work, making mistakes caused problems:

I: Would it have mattered if you'd made mistakes?
St: Yeah, we get told off.

Out of this came anger:

I: ...angry with who?
St 1&2:   The teacher...the teacher...
St 3:   Ourselves...ourselves, sir.

Also, in 'work', cooperation was cheating. In the project, by contrast mistakes involved no swallowing of feelings:

    St 1: We just . . . we just redone it.
    St 2: . . . marked it out . . .
    St 1: . . . wiped it out . . .
    St 3: . . . *rubbed* it out!

None the less, students took some 'bad habits' into cooperation. They found it hard *not* to work alone: they allocated individual tasks and got their heads down. Children who sought help were deemed intrusive. It was especially true of tense children that they were less able to free themselves from a sense of individual responsibility, which increased pressure on them.

However, these tensions were far outweighed by the positives, and students agreed with adults that behaviour was much improved:

    St 1: . . . better and differently . . .
    I: What's different?
    St 2: . . . the stories and all that and the pictures and everybody
           helping do all the writing.

It is by no means clear, but there seems here to be a relationship between different work style and different behaviour, which is tied up with cooperation. This was true even though some cooperated more than others. Even then, it still belonged to everyone:

    I: Who does it belong to?
    St: US!

There was much concern with togetherness:

    St 1: We was all helping . . . we couldn't do it . . .
    St 2: . . . we *could* do it . . .
    St 1: . . . we could do it but it was difficult . . . we had to help one
           another.

And this helping one another was actually more important then being helped by adults. I was chided as too 'bossy' for my attempts to act as 'scribe' without being invited. I should have waited to be asked, and let them have a try first, they declared.

There was clearly some learning about life and development of independence in the above, and we as adults discerned much cognitive process, which the students confirmed:

St 1: ...like you can cooperate, and then you start thinking up stories... like it was thinking caps on and start thinking...

St 2: ...we made up the stories and stories that really happened

Students actually talked and explained to one another much more than was ever normally possible, and consequently were required to define their positions. One ten-year-old boy eyed the job market nervously:

St. ...when you're doing a job you have to be interviewed, and some... and if you didn't do this work you wouldn't know what to do... 'cause then they know you can do things... and talk about them.

They also practised discrimination:

St: ...you have to think and listen to what people say... and listen and see if it's good.

As a result there were desirable consequences:

St 1: Because you get clever.

St 2: We know something... we know spellings... we know what to do and where to put it.

To one group these consequences were almost on the mountain-climbing scale:

St 1: You feel like you'll never be able to do it again, and like you don't *want* to do it again...

St 2: ...and then we try...

St 3: ...and it's easy...

All this seems far too beneficial not to be of use both in and beyond Parkside.

Conclusion and discussion

I began by making some criticisms of the behavioural objectives approach upon which much of the recent success and status of special education has been built. I went on to suggest that there were limitations to its usefulness in securing students' reintegration. Partly this is because it offers a limited curriculum and reduces opportunities for interaction with peers. The students' feedback from our project suggested furthermore that they found it rather boring, and conveyed to us a sense of plodding on through a series of tasks without perceiving interest or a point. In so far as they did make progress, this was achieved by learning to concentrate attention single-mindedly upon 'getting the right answer', and in so doing to lower their expectations of education, and perhaps of life. This is clearly undesirable; it is also poor practice.

If the evidence of our project is to be believed, it may also be the case that, carried on too long, a behavioural objectives approach may increase learned skills at the expense of an interest in learning. The adults involved in our project came also to ask themselves whether some outbreaks of 'unacceptable behaviour' were not themselves caused by feelings of boredom and by the absence of self-esteem that repetitive work can engender. Is not this questioning implied by Tomlinson (1982) in her suggestion that special education conditions its pupils for low-status employment?

By contrast, cooperative group work was a popular antidote to 'work'. For teachers it was a useful diagnostic tool, in that it identified reasons why students were unable to communicate and to negotiate, and it was also a means of counteracting these deficiencies. Behaviour clearly improved with interest and, furthermore, poor secretaries proved themselves frequently to be verbally more effective, and to be good cooperators; pupils' self-esteem was raised alongside interest. At the same time, cooperative group work was not an instant solution for children with poor secretarial skills. What it might be, however, is the means by which a diet of programmed learning might be leavened and given meaning for the bored pupil. My view would be that this could be done by offering the underachieving student the two approaches in tandem, with a clear statement why they were both used. When a good enough level of secretarial skills had developed, cooperative group work would play an increased role, and the emphasis would switch more towards developing the effectiveness of students' interaction with their peers. This in turn would offer the advantage of enhancing those active listening and communication skills that are essential for success in education.

The above brings me on finally to look at some of the implications of using cooperative group work in the mainstream. During the last year my main concern has been with support of mainstream class teachers in dealing with children with behaviour problems within their own classroom. Mainstream teachers' perceptions of difficult children seem to me to be much concerned with their own abilities to deal with what Kounin (1970) has called 'overlapping', that is, continuing to work with individuals whilst monitoring whole classes. Their ability to do this is quite naturally undermined by the demands made upon them by the wide variety of situations they have to handle. Especially when children work (as they generally do) upon individual written tasks, the teacher often becomes bogged down in combining support, the supply of vocabularly and incidental supervision. Efforts to encourage student autonomy, interaction and cooperation are, in my experience, almost as rare as in special education, and with similar consequences. Indeed, my experiences have led me to see no fundamental difference between the interest level of much of the work of primary schools and that of special schools, and little evidence of the acceptance of Tough's affirmation of the value of talk (1979). Where talk *is* valued, and where cooperation between students *is* encouraged, a fundamental change in the nature of the teacher's role occurs, which frees her to interact more effectively with individuals and to more easily supervise difficulties. Furthermore, those difficulties seem to be reduced, and a more positive classroom atmosphere ensues, in which students see themselves as empowered to take responsibility for their own learning.

I remain confident that cooperative learning styles would, if widely utilised, have significantly beneficial effects in the mainstream and in the special class for *all* participants. It is evident from the project that this chapter has sought to describe that it would be especially helpful for children seen to have individual learning needs, and would make their presence in the mainstream more secure. But, most importantly, it is only by teachers coming together actively to support one another, and to cooperate within the classroom in creating conditions that enhance and encourage effective learning, that these developments will occur. And when they do, they will acknowledge few intrinsic differences between the needs of mainstream and those of the special school.

References

Ainscow, M. and Tweddle, D. A. (1979), *Preventing Classroom Failure* (London: Fulton).
Barnes, D., Britton, J. and Rosen, H. (1969), *Language, the Learner and the School* (Harmondsworth: Penguin).
Britton, J. (1970), *Language and Learning* (Harmondsworth; Penguin).
DES (1978), *Special Educational Needs* (Warnock Report) (London: HMSO).
Elliott, J. and Adelman, C. (1976), *Innovation at the Classroom Level, Unit 28, E203* (Milton Keynes: Open University).
Hockaday, F. (1984), 'Collaborative learning with young children', *Educational Studies*, **10**(3), 237–42.

Johnson, R. T. and Johnson, D. W. (1983) 'Effects of cooperative competitive and individualistic learning experience on social development', *Exceptional Children* **49** (4), 323-9.

Johnson D. W. and Johnson R. T. (1986), 'Mainstreaming and co-operative learning strategies, *Exceptional Children*, **52** (6), 553-61.

Kounin, J. (1970), *Discipline and Group Management in Classrooms*, (New York: Rinehart & Winston).

Rosen, H. and Rosen, C. (1973), *The Language of Primary School Children* (Harmondsworth: Penguin).

Tomlinson, S. (1982), *A Sociology of Special Education* (London: RKP).

Tough, J. (1979), *Talk for Teaching and Learning* ((London: Schools Council).

Yeomans, A. (1983), 'Collaborative group work in primary and secondary schools', *Durham and Newcastle Research Review*, **10** (5), 99-105.

CHAPTER 10

Developing New Approaches Towards Assessment

Barry Ainsworth

Within this chapter I wish to argue the importance and relevance of learner participation in assessment. It seems to me that for many years teachers have taken it upon themselves to assess the quality of learning without considering the view of the learner. Tests and other mechanical means of investigating progress and attainment have traditionally excluded the opinions of the learner in the interpretation of results. It is as if, as teachers, we have felt that we know what is best for a pupil. We therefore base our teaching and material resources on the assumption that what appears best for an individual pupil is somehow subsumed within our knowledge of how individuals learn.

Recent emphasis on assessment has introduced the notion of contextual analyses in the evaluation of the performance of the individual (e.g. Broadfoot, 1986; Ainscow and Tweddle, 1988). The assessment of pupils is beginning to be considered as a complex process involving the investigation of external and internal influences that may affect the performance of the individual child. It could be said, therefore, that assessment is now being focused on appraising the mismatches that occur between the learner and the learning environment.

Through assessment of this kind the data collected during the appraisal of performance have their roots in the interaction between these internal and external factors. The interchanges that occur between pupil and teacher, pupil and pupil, or pupil and materials, often reflect this interaction. It therefore seems appropriate to say that the assessment of pupil performance forms part of the wider study of the classroom as a learning environment for the individual.

The adaptation and development of teaching and learning methods have always relied to a greater or lesser degree upon the accurate assessment of the learning environment. However, on a philosophical level, learning environments can be altered by the flutter of a butterfly's wing. For example, the weather, the absence of a pupil, a change in the timetable – these everyday occurrences can all have their effects. Environments do not remain static; they constantly change due to influences both from within and from external sources. It follows therefore that any evaluation of the classroom as a learning environment is unlikely to be 100 per cent accurate, and planned strategies for learning need to be regularly and constantly reviewed, I would argue jointly, by pupil and teacher.

The nature of assessment

Over the past ten years there has been much conjecture on the development of assessment as a continuous process. This is appropriate since circumstances both internal and external can change and different learning needs become apparent. It is therefore important to qualify what I mean by assessment. Assessment in the sense that I have been arguing is a term used to describe a gathering of information that is used to assist the continuous adaptation of learning environments, in order, through the curriculum, to establish real progress for the individual. The gathering of information, the care taken in interpreting that information and the qualitative nature of the learning strategies that arise from such an analysis are, however, only a 'snapshot' in the process of continuous learning. It therefore becomes imperative that 'the snapshot' is looked at in retrospect to see if the 'image' is still a 'good likeness'.

This analogy to photography can be explored further. There are some people who appear to be photogenic, so that regardless of the situation in which the photograph is taken they always appear in good light. Assessment can examine learners within a learning environment that because of 'photogenic' attributes seems on the surface to appear 'in good light'. We must be careful therefore to ascertain if such learning contexts are really as they seem to be for the individual. In truth, the only way that this can be achieved is to involve the learner in taking his/her own 'snapshot' and to enable the development of sufficient independence so that positive self-appraisal can be used by enabling the learner to 'focus the camera'.

In relation to the ever-changing learning environment, the only people able to establish whether the environment suits their needs are individual pupils. Pupils always remain a part of the learning environment, even though this environment may alter, for instance by moving through the different phases of education. This is not to say that learners remain constant. Pupils may change in attitude and ability because of external and internal influences. Nevertheless, they remain a part of an individual and personal learning environment throughout their schooling.

The development of a whole school approach can lead to an under-standing that the individual is worthy of equal opportunity within the school community. If equal opportunity is nurtured it becomes possible for the individual to feel supported whilst being involved in the continuous appraisal of his/her performance. In the case of a pupil with special needs this may lead to participation in the construction of learning strategies, as a consequence of which more positive attitudes can be developed. It is difficult to see how pupils can 'fail' if they have had some active involvement in deciding the nature of their learning objectives within the curriculum.

It follows therefore that, in order to establish the 'worth' of individual performance and the quality of the learning taking place, a method of assessment is required that can address the problems of a constantly changing context and assist the learner to understand and adapt.

Evaluating the learning environment

Scientific or statistical approaches, which deal in finite terms by attempting to quantify an area under research, use comparative terms, often at a given point of time. Therefore they often address the problem of defining performance by removing the assessed out of one context into another. For example, the use of a norm-referenced test often creates its own context, which bears little relationship to the individual's usual learning context. Therefore such assessments leave out an essential part of the context of a learning environment, namely the individual's ability to adapt to change.

A more suitable method for assessing the quality of education and therefore the quality of the personal learning environment lies within a 'natural' response to evaluation (Iano, 1986; Bridges et al., 1986).

Here the evaluator and the subject of the evaluation form part of the learning context. Assessment is therefore seen as a process of identifying areas that appear to affect the quality of what is taking place, continuously over a period of time.

I believe it is through assessment of the kind that I am describing that participation between the learner and the teacher should lead to natural data from which grounded theories will grow and lead to a better understanding of the strengths and weaknesses within a context. Therefore the contextual nature of the investigation will include within its boundaries the learner and the teacher.

Such natural forms of assessment are similar in many ways to recent developments in naturalistic research (e.g. Bridges *et al.*, 1986). Both rely upon the experience of the teacher and the learner as participators in the process. The nature of the data is descriptive in both cases and the interpretation of the information is subjective. This therefore allows for further interaction between the assessor and the assessed.

A strategy for assessment

As part of my work as an advisory teacher I have been developing a method of evaluation that is similar in many ways to these recent developments in assessment and research. The aim is to identify the nature of contextual problems for individual children experiencing learning difficulties in mainstream classrooms. The method itself was and is used to assist in the assessment of the learning environment alongside individual children and teachers. This method of assessment came to be the focus of an evaluation because of the growing concern of a group of support teachers about the difficulties experienced when gathering the perceptions of teachers and pupils about their teaching/learning environments.

Traditionally, teachers have been asked to write 'reports' when a child becomes a cause for concern in order for the concern to be qualified often for another professional, possibly the headteacher or maybe an external agency such as the psychological service. Due mainly to the constraints of time, such reports tend to be at the best extremely detailed but a little 'fuzzy' or at the worst a brief summary coupled to a list of normative test scores.

It is my opinion that all teachers have within their heads a 'standardised' reference of children with which they compare the individual child. In other words, if, for instance, an infant teacher has experienced the teaching of 6-year-old children over a period of time, s/he will have an imaginary 'average' six year old in his/her head. If s/he becomes concerned about an individual child it is often because that child is significantly different from this 'average'. Therefore what appears to be needed is a way of qualifying the perceptions of teachers in order to establish a way forward alongside the child. In practice, what often happens is that class teachers do not seem to believe their own perceptions and look for suitable 'published tests' with which they can confirm their opinions.

My colleagues and I began to look at ways in which the experience of teachers could be utilised in assessment in such a way as to 'tap' the classroom teachers' professional experience in order to have a greater understanding of a problem within their classrooms.

Table 10.1 Guidelines for informal assessment

EXPRESSIVE LANGUAGE
Articulation
Vocabularly
Sentence construction
Expression

RECEPTIVE LANGUAGE
Comprehension of instructions
Understanding of words
Memory for oral information

BASIC SKILLS
Fine coordination and manipulation
Drawing
Writing
Numeracy
Reading

ATTITUDE TO LEARNING
Concentration and the ability to organise
Approach to learning
Attention and distractability

BEHAVIOUR
Temperament
Attitude to teachers
Attitude to peers

SOCIAL INTEGRATION
Participation in class activities
Acceptance by peers
Desire to mix

GENERAL DEVELOPMENT
Gross motor skills
Maturity
Response to new situations

We started by gathering together a list of criteria that we hoped would assist teachers in qualifying their perceptions of the child. It was hoped that the list would utilise observation within the classroom, and eventually develop perceptions about an individual child based on professional experience. The list was presented to individual teachers. The teachers were then asked to write a sentence or two about how they felt about a child in relation to each heading on the list (Table 10.1).

The response to this approach was extremely varied. Some teachers felt that it was sufficient to write 'poor', or 'satisfactory'. Other teachers would produce documents that would run to 1500 words. Put another way, the quality and quantity of the response to this list of learning areas were patchy and at best very time-consuming.

The wheel

A solution to this problem was adapted from a chart used by coffee tasters to assess the quality of a blend, which I happened to see in a magazine advertisement. By substituting the criteria of the coffee taster for the criteria used to gather the perceptions of teachers, it became possible for an individual teacher to represent his/her perceptions of an individual child pictorially. The chart consisted of a wheel of seven concentric circles with 24 spokes. Each spoke was given a heading from the list in Table 10.1. It was explained to the teachers that the centre of the chart denoted 'weakness' whereas the outer circle denoted 'strength'. Because the teachers were being asked for their subjective perceptions of what appeared to be taking place, the chart could be completed in a matter of minutes.

The support teachers could then negotiate with the school to find some time for each teacher to describe their perceptions in terms of the strengths and weaknesses pictorially represented on the chart. The pictorial nature of the chart allowed for comments on comparability between different areas. For example, a teacher might have denoted 'concentration' as a weaker area then 'distraction'. The discussion centred on this difference often led to a clearer definition of what appeared to be taking place.

The information obtained through using the chart as an agenda, when analysed, often led to some further strategies to assist the child in his/her learning.

In order to establish how accurate the teachers' perceptions were, the child would also be involved by being asked to describe his/her learning environment. Depending on the age of the child, the same criteria or similar but adapted criteria would be used as an agenda. Both the teacher and the child would then review the information so that a dialogue could be established and further action could be jointly agreed upon. In many cases the parents would also be involved and their perceptions would be added to the information.

Evaluation

As I attempted to evaluate this method of assessment, a number of interesting points emerged. For example, it quickly became apparent that by questioning it was possible to lead the teacher and the pupil to give information that, instead of being a true reflection of their perceptions, was in fact information that they expected was being sought by the assessment. This was particularly apparent with younger pupils, who tended to want to give 'answers' which they felt the teacher required. To combat this, the support teachers made efforts to become more experienced and skilled in counselling techniques, which enabled pupils and teachers to offer information that reflected their 'true' perceptions.

My research into the assessment method looked at different forms of information contained in the transcripts of disscussions centred upon the 'wheel'. I tried to establish which information was more readily utilised in deciding upon agreed further action. It became evident that it was not easy to determine which form of information was more relevant, in that sense, than any other when looking for ways forward. This was because the information was by its nature individual. Therefore it was possible to use as much of the information as necessary to decide upon further action. Through this individuality, it also became possible to involve the pupil in the decision-making process. Consequently, realistic strategies were arrived at. In addition, a sense of 'decision ownership' was established in the teacher and the learner.

However, it was also established that any further action agreed between the learner and the teacher would have to be reviewed after an appropriate length of time so that relevance could be maintained. This has led to the development of 'self-support' within the classroom.

Despite this, many teachers express the opinion that the involvement of an external agency to coordinate the initial assessment and the review of action is necessary. They feel this for two main reasons:

(1) Pupils may not see the support teacher as a 'real' teacher. Consequently, because they sense that the support teacher does not have a

vested interest in the school, they are more willing to discuss their perceptions of their own learning.

(2) Class teachers may also feel more secure discussing their perceptions of the learner and the classroom with someone who is not a member of the staff of the school. Perhaps this is because teachers are traditionally reticent about admiting 'inadequacies' with working colleagues.

Conclusion

The work that I have carried out has led me to believe that learning should be primarily owned by the learner. As teachers, we are really in the position of designing learning environments that, as far as possible are flexible enough for the learner to adapt to as an individual. This, I believe, is a central requirement of good teaching practice.

It has become evident, through using a natural method of assessment, that special educational needs do not require anything 'special' in the way of different curricula or resources. I would go so far as to say that the form of assessment that has been described in this chapter is nothing more or less than what every teacher accomplished throughout the school year. At its simplest, it is a gathering of information, a review with the pupil and the agreement of a way forward. As teachers we are constantly doing this every day when we decide what a pupil should do next. By considering the views of the pupil more in that decision-making process, we should surely be able to cater for the educational needs of all children.

There seems to be a common thread running through many recent developments in the educational world. This common thread has much to do with the notion of decision ownership. Teacher appraisal, pupil assessment, research methodology and the management of schools are all areas where natural responses appear to lead to a sense of ownership on the part of the individual. I believe that natural methods should be nurtured in the area of assessment so that a shared response to problems will lead to positive attitudes in this time of great educational change.

Much of what I believe can be summed up within the idea of action research. Elliott (1981) defines action research as 'the study of a social situation with a view to improving the quality of the action within it'. He then clarifies the purpose as follows:

> It aims to feed practical judgement in concrete situations, and the validity of the theories it generates depends not so much on scientific tests of truth as on their usefulness in helping people to act more intelli-

130

gently and skilfully. In action research theories are not validated independently and then applied to practice. They are validated through practice.

The similarities between action research and classroom-based assessment of the sort I have described are so adjacent that they could be viewed as one and the same thing.

Within the development of the National Curriculum and the recommendations for assessment included within the current documentation (DES, 1988), I see opportunities to be creative and positive about pupil participation in assessment. The guidelines for aims and objectives appear to give reasonably clear targets, which could be understood by individual pupils and therefore could assist the pupil to develop skills of self-appraisal. This in turn should help build greater confidence to consult with the teacher when confronted by new areas or difficult concepts.

References

Ainscow, M. and Tweddle, D. A. (1988) *Encouraging Classroom Success* (London: Fulton).

Bridges, D., Elliott, J. and Klass, C. (1986), 'Performance appraisal as naturalistic inquiry', *Cambridge Journal of Education*, **16**(3), 221–33.

Broadfoot, P. (ed.) (1986), *Profiles and Records of Achievement* (London: Holt, Rinehart & Winston).

DES (1978), *Special Educational Needs* (London: HMSO).

DES (1983), *Assessments and Statements of Special Needs*, Circular 1/83 (London: Department of Education and Science).

DES (1988), *Report of Task Group on Assessment* (London: Department of Education and Science).

Elliott, J. (1981), 'Action research: a framework for self evaluation in schools, Schools Council Programme 2, Teacher–Pupil Interaction and the Quality of Learning Project, Working Paper 1 (Cambridge: Cambridge Institute of Education.

Iano, R. (1986), 'The study and development of teaching', *Remedial and Special Education*, **7**(5), 50–50.

CHAPTER 11

How to Help the Ship Along: An Evaluation of Effective Support Teaching

Andy Redpath

An article appeared in the *Times Educational Supplement* in autumn 1988, in which a frustrated primary school headteacher expressed disbelief at the priorities of his school's peripatetic support teacher. He claimed that, by concentrating exclusively on the performance and capabilities of individual children, this particular special needs teacher, and perhaps others, often lose sight of wider, more pressing issues facing the school. They 'stand around talking about phonics and tests while life and death goes on. They argue about the colour of the funnel as the ship goes down' (Sedgwick, 1988).

This chapter discusses the work of one embryonic primary support service, where attempts were made to look beyond the attainments of individual children and to become involved in shaping broader, whole school policies, which affect pupil behaviour and achievement more generally. In short, helping to steer the ship, rather than arguing about the colour of the funnel! It is also an illustration of how the knowledge of special school teachers, combined with appropriate INSET, can be used to benefit their mainstream colleagues.

The need to move away from focusing solely on particular children when seeking solutions to behaviour and learning difficulties in schools is gaining increasing acceptance. Galloway (1985) and Dessent (1987) suggest that pupil performance is more likely to be influenced by such factors as teacher expectations, curriculum design and school organisation, rather than some inherent child weakness or 'deficit'. Consequently, it is argued, teachers should be in the business of encouraging all children to succeed, rather than focusing on the special needs of a few (Ainscow and Tweddle, 1988).

The project

Informed of this new perspective, and convinced of the benefit of providing help initially within schools, before considering more drastic options such as referral for special education, 'Urban Borough' decided to set up a primary support service in September 1987. The service would be run jointly by the schools psychological service and the borough special school for children with emotional and behavioural difficulties, 'Woodvale'. The pilot scheme was to involve one support teacher serving two primary schools, and initially operate for a year, during which time it would be evaluated before a decision was taken regarding its continuation or possible expansion. As a student at the Cambridge Institute of Education, on secondment from the borough, I was asked to complete the evaluation.

At the time this seemed a daunting, yet exciting, proposition. As a practising teacher for a number of years, I was aware of the potential difficulties facing 'outsiders' trespassing in the private domain of the classroom. Traditionally, teachers are suspicious of researchers and their motives. Their findings are often perceived as being unduly critical and out of touch with the realities of daily classroom survival. Yes, it was tempting to retreat into the safe haven of a library and complete some esoteric essay that would equally satisfy course requirements!

Conversely, it was good to feel that the secondment could actually serve a purpose over and above personal self-fulfilment, and that the commitment of the school and local education authority to staff development be seen to reap tangible rewards. Also, feelings of guilt might be assuaged if less privileged colleagues benefited in some way from my brief exposure to academic study. Therefore, to be successful the study would have to be relevant and accessible, or in computer parlance 'user friendly', whilst at the same time maintaining intellectual rigour. Given that I had been allowed time away from school to study, it was important that there was evidence of having read widely and applying new ideas effectively. Writing for an audience comprising one's colleagues is demanding, and a great stimulation to produce worthwhile results!

As deputy head of Woodvale, in people's minds I would inevitably be linked with the school's support service, so from the outset there could be no notion of 'distanced objectivity'. I was very much a part of the process I was examining. However, as well as using my own observations, data were gathered from other perspectives, by interviewing headteachers, teachers, educational psychologist and parents, and by introducing a classroom activity with two classes of children. This method of cross-referencing has been described by Denzin (1978) and Cohen and Manion (1980), and is widely referred to as 'triangulated verification'. Viewpoints from different participants are sought and compared in an attempt to seek a clearer understanding of what is happening. The great strength of this approach lies in the fact that it demystifies the research process, it is easily understood and, by involving them, it encourages teachers to reflect upon their own practice.

To avoid excessive reliance on introspective reports, I combined data from observations and interviews with the results of a questionnaire distributed in the two schools. In addition, related documentation was examined, and current literature concerning support work referred to throughout the text, linking it with wider theory.

It was fortunate that the establishment of the support service coincided with the return to Woodvale, in September 1987, of another teacher from a year's secondment at the Cambridge Institute of Education. A teacher of considerable experience, 'Mr Briant' had worked at Woodvale for ten years, and had been involved in liaising with mainstream schools, supporting children who attended Woodvale part-time. Part of the course at Cambridge had been concerned with the integration of children with special needs, and discussed some of the skills required by support teachers in order to make integration a success. Thus it is fair to say that Mr Briant possessed the necessary experience, enriched by the study of recent theory, to act as a support teacher, and this enhanced the prospects of the support service.

Hence, the aims of the Woodvale Primary Support Service were clearly set out in advance, and reflect thinking that suggest a child's behaviour and performance at school are inextricably linked to the classroom context within which they occur. Consequently, an important aim of the service was to reduce the need to withdraw children from classrooms and schools, by refining classroom management techniques used by the teacher. This would increase his/her confidence 'in their ability to handle disruptive behaviour in a positive and flexible way'. At the wider school level, the support service envisaged being involved in an examination of the curriculum, in setting up school-based in-service training, and in the development of school policies on behaviour management.

Research design

The success of the service could in large part be measured in relation to the furtherance of these aims. It was proposed that evaluation should take two, and possibly three, forms:

(i) an evaluation of behavioural change in students referred to the school's support service;
(ii) an evaluation of teachers' responses to the intervention;
(iii) an evaluation of students' responses to the intervention.

This study worked from the premise that these three aspects are essentially interrelated and form a process of interaction taking place in the classroom. Research (e.g. Croll and Moses, 1985) suggests that teachers' perceptions play an important part in defining a pupil's behaviour and level of achievement. Thus there was an attempt to examine classroom processes, and the extent to which they were enriched by support service intervention. The approach is best described as 'qualitative' (Elliott, 1981) and sought to add greater understanding to the nature of support offered, rather than 'prove' causal relationships.

The research officially commenced on 1 February 1988; however, most of the data were gathered during the summer term, April–June. Given that the study commenced after the Woodvale Primary Support Service was already in operation, 'before' and 'after' measures of referred pupil's progress would not have been possible, and this could be regarded as a limitation of any findings. However, if ultimately there is a reduction in withdrawal and referral of children to Wood-vale, that in itself could be regarded as an indication of support service success.

It was anticipated that the direction of the research would become clearer as the programme evolved. Consequently, there was no set schedule for the study, rather an 'emerging design'. What seemed important, initially, was to gain a general picture of how the support teacher spent his day; how he related to teachers in the host schools; and the methods he used to improve the behaviour of those children who had been referred for special help. This involved 'shadowing' Mr

Briant for several days. It occurred to me that the support teacher must have experienced feelings of trepidation similar to my own when he first entered classrooms and schools. The fact that he had succeeded in establishing a constructive relationship with staff at the two schools where he worked paved the way for my ease of access. Also, there seemed to be some advantage in being a fellow teacher, familiar with, and sympathetic to, the problems facing classroom colleagues. After all, I wasn't a proper researcher!

Support in action

It soon became clear that the support teacher involved himself in the class by working with groups of children, not necessarily restricting his attentions to any particular referred child. This had the advantage of not drawing attention to that child, and reducing the possibility of comment from peers. Modification of the pupil's learning materials could occur, enabling him/her to complete the tasks set and make a contribution to the lesson. However, the main concern was with providing access, rather than setting up a separate learning programme.

An example of this approach was observed with a second-year junior class at one of the schools. The children discussed a topic in groups, wrote down ideas, and then presented their views to the rest of the class. Mr Briant moved freely between the groups, enabling children experiencing problems to participate. As well as providing help with written work and spelling, he encouraged them to participate socially. On one occasion he jovially marched out a boy to the front of the class who had been reluctant to present his work. The pupil succeeded and was clearly pleased at having done so. Mr Briant often sat near pupils who were having difficulty with concentration, jollying them along and maintaining their interest.

In discussing approaches to team teaching, Thomas (1986) has described how it is beneficial for one teacher to maintain the flow of the lesson, while the second adult gives individual help to children experiencing difficulty. The support teacher performed the latter role, being alert to the aims of the class teacher, and reinforcing or explaining them to groups of children. Teachers who worked closely with Mr Briant stressed that an important feature of the way he worked was that he did not 'take over the class' but tuned into what they were doing and enhanced the process.

Because of his non-threatening manner, Mr Briant's views were welcomed by staff, and he was able to become involved in devising strategies for improving the behaviour of all pupils around the school. Strong evidence emerged from interviews and questionnaires to suggest that not only teachers of referred pupils, but staff generally, felt they had improved their skills at handling children who present difficult behaviour. Parents of the seven referred pupils seemed pleased with the progress of their children. Since the arrival of the support teacher it was claimed there had been fewer negative reports from school.

Pupil perspectives

Not drawing attention to individual pupils in need of help seemed extremely valuable, in so far as it avoided stigma and possible unfavourable peer attention. But how could adults be sure this was being achieved? Children are usually quite shrewd at detecting teacher motives and expectations. Bearing in mind 'triangulated verification', it seemed useful to find out how all the pupils in a class perceived Briant and his work.

This was achieved by dividing a class at each school into groups and asking them to brainstorm ideas around three questions: 'Who is he?' 'What is he like?' 'What sort of things does he do?' The task was introduced as a detective game, groups having to identify a large silhouette of Mr Briant. Once this had been done, they could then write down their ideas, cut them out and stick them on the silhouette.

At one school, a class of first-year juniors completed the exercise, with most children identifying the silhouette correctly. However, one sub-group of pupils did feel it could be the school caretaker, and were allowed to list their comments separately. There were four groups of five children, each with its own silhouette (A1 size) on grey sugar paper. Some of the recurring sentiments referring to Mr Briant were as follows:

- *Who is he?*
  he is a teacher
  he is half a teacher
- *What is he like?*
  he is very tall
  he has a beard
  he is funny
  helpful
  kind

a very nice man
has big smile
is happy
good
clever
very bright
is not noisy
● *What does he do?*
he says kind things to people
he helps people
tells jokes
he works hard, the same as we do
reads us stories
helps us to do our work
gives us sweets if we are good
helps people to spell
helps us with our work
gives us presents
he likes to work
tidies up for us (perhaps he was the school caretaker after all!)

These comments seem to recognise the varied nature of the support teacher's work. Qualities mentioned by staff, such as humour and a friendly, warm manner, seem equally important to the children. Also, the helping or enabling role is emphasised. There is no mention of the referred child who Mr Briant was officially intervening to help; rather he had joined the class to 'help us'.

I was more apprehensive about introducing the exercise with the younger, middle infants class at the second school. I envisaged that they would find it more difficult to express ideas and write them down. However, the class teacher proved extremely helpful. On her advice we decided to cut up the paper into small strips, encourage children to draw pictures conveying their ideas, and, when asked, write down words for children to copy. This class was split into five groups. The end-product from all groups proved to be extremely stimulating; children covered every square inch of the paper with pictures and writing.

The comments were very similar to those of the class at the first school, but there was an additional aspect of Mr Briant's approach that some younger children found significant. That was the tactile nature of his relationship with them: 'He tickles us . . . he tickles us and picks us up . . . he shakes my hand . . . sometimes he pulls ears and shakes my hand.' They also remarked that 'sometimes he is cross', particularly with one boy in the class, Tommy. Tommy was not the pupil referred for help from Mr Briant and, as with the first class, children thought he was there to help them all. Pictures portrayed flag-waving, smiling faces, and outstretched arms, generally conveying a feeling of good humour and happiness. However, alongside one beaming Mr Happy, was found a pirate with facial features completely obscured by beard!

Pupils in both classes clearly enjoyed having Mr Briant in their lessons. Claims from teachers that 'borderline pupils', who had not been referred, were also helped by the support teacher seemed well founded. Mr Briant noticed children around the school and struck up a good rapport with them. Teachers confirmed how he was liked and respected by pupils, and the head of one school described how he 'jollied children along' and had nicknames for them.

Personal skills

It was evident that the success of the project rested heavily upon the personal skills of the support teacher. He had built a credible image amongst the broad range of staff at the two schools. Davies and Davies (1988) have listed several interdependent factors instrumental in establishing credibility and sustaining it, of which four were particularly relevant to the success of the Woodvale support service: consultation, positive professional exchange, responsive and flexible approaches, and perspective and humour. To these can be added four others that emerged during the course of the study: rapport with children, encouraging ownership of change, sensitivity to micro-political processes, and counselling skills.

Consultation and negotiation

The support teacher himself stressed the need to seek teachers' views and negotiate a course of action with them. It was important to listen to colleagues, recognise their perceptions as valid, and empathise with their problems. This process of consultation was extended to children who the support teacher felt were not always aware of teacher expectations or of the consequences of their own behaviour.

Positive professional exchange

A specific 'problem-solving' approach was adopted that encouraged the class teacher and support teacher to tackle a mutual problem together. Emphasising that he was 'joining with' teachers, the support teacher deliberately referred to 'us' or 'we' when describing a problem or discussing its possible solution with a teacher. He felt it was important to build mutual respect and 'hold back on instant solutions'.

Responsive and flexible approaches

There was an emphasis on working from the teacher's position, and having a 'feel for the situation' existing in the classroom. It was apparent that teachers were more favourably inclined towards change that builds on existing practice. Teaching styles are essentially personal and different. By understanding the nuances of the teaching process and enhancing it, progress was more likely to be made.

Humour and perspective

Staff in both schools looked forward to the support teacher coming in and spoke warmly about him in his absence. He had established a highly visible presence, based upon humour and 'jokey informality' in dealing with colleagues. Several teachers felt that the success of the project was largely due to the support teacher's amenable and jovial personality. 'He cheers me up when I feel frustrated,' commented one headteacher.

Rapport with children

A common complaint amongst teachers is that those who offer advice frequently 'cannot do the job themselves' or are 'no good with kids'. The support teacher's obvious ability to communicate well with children was central to teachers recognising his skills, respecting his judgement and accepting his advice. Casually acknowledging children around the school, engaging them in conversation, and offering praise and encouragement, were essential features of his approach, which aided children in developing a positive self-image. Popularity with the children, based upon respect, allowed classroom intervention by the support teacher to be an enriching experience, rather than a disruptive one that brought with it new problems of discipline and control. In short, acceptance by pupils facilitated the development of a positive relationship between the class teacher and the support teacher.

Encouraging ownership of change

The support teacher said, 'It is not enough to say what is wrong; involving teachers in a process of change is important to make it last or stick.' Developing this theme, Dessent (1987) has referred to the need for ordinary schools and teachers to 'own' their problems and solutions. In relation to the implementation of SNAP, Muncey and Ainscow (1983) have stressed the need for teachers to feel they are involved in defining problems and formulating solutions, then they are more likely to implement any changes agreed. Recognising this approach, the support teacher emphasised that selling solutions, however worthy, was not constructive: 'You must not try to impose ideas and become involved in battles you cannot win.'

Sensitivity to 'micropolitical' processes

Hoyle (1982) has referred to the existence in schools of micropolitical processes whereby individuals and groups informally exert influence on decision-making. This is characterised 'more by coalitions than by departments, by strategies rather than by enacted rules, by influence rather than by power, and by knowledge rather than by status.' Recognising this perspective, the support teacher stressed the need to 'stand back and be observant' and be wary of 'identifying with particular factions or groups in schools'. To do so would 'restrict the ability to negotiate with a variety of people'.

By maintaining circumspection and distance, the support teacher achieved informal acceptance in both staff rooms, and gained respect from the broad spectrum of staff in the two schools.

Counselling skills

The above factors may best be viewed as interdependent 'elements'. Underpinning them all, and perhaps fundamental to the success of the project, were the skills of an effective counsellor.

In relation to the personality of a successful counsellor, Hamblin (1974) has stressed three important qualities. The first is 'empathy' or the ability to 'feel into' a person or situation. Hamblin states that this is more than an intellectual exercise; it is a 'type of momentary identification'. The second quality is 'spontaneity and genuineness' – the capacity to relate honestly and reveal oneself as 'one human being to another'. Linked with this, it seems necessary to possess a feeling of self-worth. Finally, the counsellor must have the capacity to show a 'non-threatening, safe and non-possessive warmth'. The support teacher's acceptance in the classrooms and staff room of each school was in large part due to his ability to listen to colleagues, show emphathy, demonstrate warmth and genuineness, build on their ideas, and encourage them to seek solutions within their own capabilities. Staff at both schools valued his company, regarding him as a sympathetic ear with whom they could talk freely and openly.

These skills were crucial to the success of the Woodvale support service. It would seem that the expertise necessary for this 'counselling' role is quite different from that traditionally employed by teachers working with children on an individual withdrawal basis. Teachers entering schools to offer support and advice need to be aware of a sophisticated range of approaches, which has implications for staff recruitment and training. However, where these skills are in evidence and put to effective use amongst colleagues, an atmosphere of mutual cooperation and trust can flourish. Where this prevails, staff are likely to do more than simply listen to new ideas; they will develop their own professional skills and resources, making the 'whole school' approach to special educational needs a more realistic prospect.

Concluding comment

After its initial year, the primary support service was well established in both schools. The success of the Woodvale support service rested heavily upon the personal skills of the support teacher. The support teacher had climbed on board the ship and become a valued member of the crew. The extent to which he could help steer the ship obviously depended on the particular circumstances prevailing in each school, but future prospects looked good. The borough is interested in making the service available to more schools, but current staffing difficulties inhibit expansion.

At a more local level, one of the benefits of the evaluation has been to provide a starting point for other staff based at Woodvale who are involved in offering mainstream support to reflect on their current practice. Since returning to school, when I am approached in the staff room by colleagues, rather than ask, 'Did you have a nice year off?' it is more usual for them to enquire, 'Have you got a spare copy of your evaluation?'

142

References

Ainscow, M. and Tweddle, D. A. (1988), *Encouraging Classroom Success* (London: Fulton).

Cohen, L. and Manion, L. (1980), *Research Methods in Education* (London: Croom Helm).

Croll, P. and Moses, D. (1985), *One in Five – The Assessment and Incidence of Special Educational Needs* (London: RKP).

Davies, J. D. and Davies, P. (1988), 'Developing credibility as a support and advisory teacher', *Support for Learning*, **3**(1), February.

Denzin, N. (1978), *The Research Act* (London: McGraw Hill).

Dessent, T. (1987), *Making the Ordinary School Special* (Brighton: Falmer Press).

Elliott, J. (1981) 'Action research: A framework for self-evaluation in schools' (Cambridge Institute of Education, mimeo).

Galloway, D. (1985), *Schools, Pupils and Special Educational Needs* (London: Croom Helm).

Hamblin, D. H. (1974), *The Teacher and Counselling* (London: Blackwell).

Hoyle, E. (1982), 'The micropolitics of educational organisation', *Educational Administration and Management*, **10**(2).

Muncey, J. and Ainscow, M. (1983), 'Launching SNAP in Coventry', *Special Education Forward Trends*, **10**(3), 8–12.

Sedgwick, F. (1988), 'Sort this one out . . .', *Times Educational Supplement*, 28 October.

Thomas, G. (1986), 'Integrating personnel in order to integrate children', *Support for Learning*, **1**(1), February.

CHAPTER 12

School-Based Inquiry

Mel Ainscow

This final chapter provides some suggestions for readers who wish to carry out investigations into aspects of their own practice. The content is based upon material used on advanced courses for experienced teachers at the Cambridge Institute of Education (Ainscow *et al.*, 1987).

Lewis and Munn (1987) suggest that teachers tend to do research for one of the following reasons:

(1) To *monitor* and influence the direction of new developments.
(2) To *try to find out* what is actually going on, recognising that what actually occurs is not always the same as what is thought to occur.
(3) To *evaluate* what is already taking place.

They suggest that:

> The overall aim of these kinds of research is usually to provide some systematic and reliable information that can be used as a basis for action. Instead of relying upon intuition and value judgements in making decisions, the individual teacher, the department or the school staff as a whole can use carefully collected evidence to feed into the decision-making process.

There are clearly varying levels at which this might be applied. For example:

○ An individual teacher may have identified a problem, an interest, or a concern within his or her own classroom and wish to find out more to resolve a dilemma. This may be related to an individual child, a group of children, an aspect of the curriculum or classroom management.

○ A group of teachers may wish to review a range of alternative curriculum proposals to judge their likely impact on practice.

○ A school staff may need to evaluate practice, performance and policy in teaching and in administration.

○ There may be a need to provide evidence and analysis of the school's programme for management purposes or to inform the LEA, school governors, parents and others.

○ There is also likely to be a need to interpret and to assess information coming into schools from a variety of outside sources (e.g. central government, the local education authority).

Whatever the purpose, school-based inquiries can be formulated by addressing the following questions:

● What do you want to know? (and why?)
● How are you going to find out?
● What does this tell you?
● What are you going to do about it?

In helping course participants to find suitable areas for investigation, we suggest that they consider the following points:

- First, attempt to provide an outline of your idea.
- Then consider the purposes that are to be served by such an inquiry.
- Reflect upon other potential influences: the children, your colleagues (including those who may not share your concern), as well as other professional contacts.
- The available literature is another important consideration. This can be of two kinds – that which helps refine the investigation and that which helps with the process of undertaking the research.
- Another crucial issue is that of access: is the research going to require visits to other classrooms, other schools or seeing people who may be difficult to contact? What implications will this have for planning?
- Finally, it is also worth reflecting upon the time-scale, especially whether or not the proposal is manageable within the time available.

In addition, a useful source of help in formulating research questions is Lewis and Munn (1987).

Having formulated the focus of the investigation by working out a problem or question, the next stage must be to design some methods for gathering and analysing information. The notes that follow provide some information that should be of help in making these decisions and draw attention to some issues of importance. They also provide some suggested sources of further information.

Code of ethics

Given that most forms of inquiry involve other people, their behaviour and their points of view, it is important to consider the ethical implications of the information that is gathered. John Elliott (1981) suggests that the key issues are:

● confidentiality
● negotiation
● control.

He argues that confidential information should not be released until this has been agreed with the person or persons to whom it belongs.

In carrying out an inquiry, therefore, it is necessary to think carefully about how this process of negotiation can be undertaken. Table 12.1 is a code of ethics from Kemmis and McTaggart (1981), which should be helpful in this respect.

Table 12.1 Code of ethics for researchers

Observe protocol: Take care to ensure that the relevant persons, committees and authorities have been consulted, informed and that the necessary permission and approval has been obtained.

Involve participants: Encourage others who have a stake in the improvement you envisage to shape the form of the work.

Negotiate with those affected: Not everyone will want to be directly involved; your work should take account of the responsibilities and wishes of others.

Report progress: Keep the work visible and remain open to suggestions so that unforeseen and unseen ramifications can be taken account of; colleagues must have the opportunity to lodge a protest to you.

Obtain explicit authorization before you observe: For the purposes of recording the activities of professional colleagues or others (the observation of your own students falls outside this imperative provided that your aim is the improvement of teaching and learning).

Obtain explicit authorization before you examine files, correspondence or other documentation: Take copies only if specific authority to do this is obtained.

Negotiate descriptions of people's work: Always allow those described to challenge your accounts on the grounds of fairness, relevance and accuracy.

Negotiate accounts of others' points of view (e.g. in accounts of communication): Always allow those involved in interviews, meetings and written exchanges to require amendments which enhance fairness, relevance and accuracy.

Table 12.1 Continued.

Obtain explicit authorization before using quotations: Verbatim transcripts, attributed observations, excerpts of audio and video recordings, judgements, conclusions or recommendations in reports (written or to meetings).

Negotiate reports for various levels of release: Remember that different audiences demand different kinds of reports; what is appropriate for an informal verbal report to a faculty meeting may not be appropriate for a staff meeting, a report to council, a journal article, a newspaper, a newsletter to parents; be conservative if you cannot control distribution.

Accept responsibility for maintaining confidentiality.

Retain the right to report your work: Provided that those involved are satisfied with the fairness, accuracy and relevance of accounts which pertain to them; and that the accounts do not unnecessarily expose or embarrass those involved; then accounts should not be subject to veto or be sheltered by prohibitions of confidentiality.

Make your principles of procedure binding and known: All of the people involved in your action research project must agree to the principles before the work begins; others must be aware of their rights in the process.

Source: Kemmis and McTaggart (1981).

Choosing methods

In choosing appropriate methods for gathering information, the following issues need to be kept in mind:

● Do the methods relate to my research question?
● Are they feasible in the time available?
● Am I aware of their strengths and limitations?
● Will they be acceptable to those involved in the investigation?
● Are they too disruptive?

It is impossible to provide a comprehensive list of possible methods of inquiry but it is likely that, in most cases, school-based investigations will involve one or more of the following:

(i) *Narrative approaches to observation*
(e.g. field notes; anecdotal records; diaries)
Sources:
Hopkins (1985), pages 59/61, 64/66
Bell (1987), Chapter 9
Hook (1981), Chapter 6

(ii) *Systematic observation*
(e.g. checklists; rating scales; event and time sampling)
Sources:
Hopkins (1985), pages 90–103
Bell (1987), Chapter 10
Hook (1981), Chapters 3, 4 and 5

(iii) *Tests*
(e.g. norm and criterion referenced)
Sources:
Cohen and Manion (1985), Chapter 6
Popham (1981), Chapter 2
Evans (1984), Chapter 4
(iv) *Interviews*
(e.g. structured and unstructured; group discussion)
Sources:
Hopkins (1985), pages 66–70
Bell (1987), Chapter 8
Hook (1981), Chapter 7
Cohen and Manion (1985), Chapter 13
(v) *Questionnaires*
Sources:
Hopkins (1985), pages 72–5
Bell (1987), Chapter 7
Hook (1981), Chapter 8
Cohen and Manion (1985), pages 103–13
(vi) *Audio-visual recordings*
(e.g. video and audio records; photography)
Sources:
Hopkins (1985), pages 61–4, 70–2, 80
Hook (1981), Chapter 11
(vii) *Documentary evidence*
(e.g. minutes of meetings; policy documents; classroom materials)
Sources:
Hopkins (1985), pages 78–9
Bell (1987), Chapter 6
Cohen and Manion (1985), Chapter 2.

Checking information

Methods of inquiry should be examined critically as they are used in order to determine the extent to which they are *valid* and *reliable*. In other words we need to consider:

● Does the method measure or describe what it set out to do? (i.e. Is it valid?)
● Does the method provide similar information on different occasions? (i.e. Is it reliable?)

In small-scale investigations it is difficult to be certain about the answers to these questions, but they should be kept in mind.

A particularly useful strategy for checking information is known as *triangulation*. Put simply this means the use of two or more sets of information to study the one event or process. It may, for example, involve comparing and contrasting information using different methods (e.g. interviews and questionnaires) or by taking account of the views of different people. There is a range of other methods for checking the trustworthiness of methods that may also be appropriate.

Sources:
Cohen and Manion (1985), Chapter 11
Elliott (1981), page 19
Skrtic (1985), pages 200–2.

Data analysis

The analysis of data can often be the most difficult aspect of an investigation. Within the approaches described here it is a process that can commence alongside data collection.

In general terms, data analysis is likely to involve the following interrelated processes:

- the mechanical tasks of data processing, e.g. sifting, analysing, collating, ordering, categorising and coding.
- making some sense of what the data is saying. This process involves the attempt to fit all the varied information into a coherent story or picture by means of a conceptual framework. A balance has to be struck between forcing the data to fit an inappropriate framework (thus having to omit the awkward bits) and presenting the information in such a disorganised form that it is impossible to make sense of it. Ideally, the researcher is looking for a useful conceptual framework that *illuminates, interprets, explains* and *structures* the accumulating data.
- deciding whether the evidence supports the case being made. The application of such considerations as *reliability* and *validity* is again important here.
- further checking may be required, so one decision may well be to go back and collect more data, perhaps in one particular area, to substantiate or disconfirm an emerging set of impressions.
- reflecting on, and learning from, the implications of the research.
- reporting and presenting the research – leading to decision-making and action on the strength of the research.

Sources:
Lincoln and Guba (1985), pages 347–8
Marshall (1981), pages 395–9
Merriam (1988), Chapters 8 and 9
Miles and Huberman (1984), Chapters 3, 4 and 5
Woods (1986), Chapters 6 and 7.

References

Ainscow, M., Conner, C. and Holly, P. (1987), *School Based Inquiry* (Cambridge: Cambridge Institute of Education).
Bell, J. (1987), *Doing Your Research Project* (Milton Keynes: Open University).
Cohen, L. and Manion, L. (1985), *Research Methods in Education* (London: Croom Helm).
Elliott, J. (1981), 'Action research: A framework for self-evaluation in schools' (Cambridge Institute of Education, mimeo).
Evans, K. M. (1984), *Planning Small Scale Research* (Slough: NFER – Nelson).
Hook, C. (1981), *Studying Classrooms* (Victoria: Deakin University Press).
Hopkins, D. (1985), *A Teacher's Guide to Classroom Research* (Milton Keynes: Open University).
Kemmis, S. and McTaggart, R. (1981), *The Action Research Planner* (Victoria: Deakin University Press).
Lewis, I. and Munn, P. (1987), *So You Want to Do Research* (Edinburgh: Scottish Council for Research in Education).
Lincoln, Y. S. and Guba, E. G. (1985), *Naturalistic Inquiry* (Beverly Hills: Sage).
Marshall, J. (1981), 'Making sense as a personal process', in P. Reason and J. Rowan (eds), *Human Inquiry* (Chichester: Wiley).
Merriam, S. B. (1988), *Case Study Research in Education* (London: Jossey-Bass).
Miles, M. B. and Huberman, A. M. (1984), *Qualitative Data Analysis* (Beverly Hills: Sage).
Popham, W. J. (1981), *Modern Educational Measurement* (New York: Prentice Hall).
Skrtic, T. M. (1985), 'Doing naturalistic research into educational organisations', in Y. S. Lincoln (ed.), *Organisational Theory and Inquiry* (Beverly Hills: Sage).
Woods, P. (1986), *Inside Schools* (London: RKP).